AF469113

COASTERS OF THE CHANNEL ISLANDS

by

Dave Hocquard

INTRODUCTION

From the earliest times, anchorages in sheltered bays were used by vessels trading to the Channel Islands. Ships would anchor as near to high water as possible, and ground as the tide receded and discharge their cargo over the side at low water. As time went by, trade increased and larger ships began trading to the islands, it was realised that ships needed more shelter and better facilities. The first breakwaters were simple affairs, just a long pile of boulders to break up the swells.

The first proper stone piers were constructed during the 18th century on the three main islands. St Helier had her first enclosed harbour on completion of North Pier in 1790 forming what is now known as the Old Harbour. The Victoria Pier was built between 1841 and 1846, while the Albert Pier was constructed between 1846 and 1853 forming what is now the main harbour. Elizabeth Castle breakwater was started in 1872 and reached its present length in 1890s giving the harbour better protection during the south westerly gales.

The last extension to St Helier Harbour for cargo only was the completion in 1979 of the present tanker berth at La Collette, able to take vessels up to 100 metres (328 feet) long.

Ronez Quarry jetty on the north coast was completed in 1903 to facilitate the export of stone to England's south coast ports and shipped its last cargo in 1978.

Until 1850 St Peter Port, Guernsey, only had the small harbour now known as the Old Harbour. A major new harbour was started in 1853 with the south arm and completed in 1867. This linked the islet on which Castle Cornet is built to the mainland of Guernsey. The North arm, better known as St Julian's Pier, was built and completed in the1870s forming the fine harbour the island has today.

St Sampsons Harbour was created from a tidal creek, which made the northern part of Guernsey a separate island during periods of high water. From the early days the harbour was mainly used for the export of granite from the many quarries in the area, and later for most of the bulk cargoes into the island.

Alderney's first pier at Braye Bay was Douglas Quay dating from 1736. The massive breakwater across the bay was started in 1847 and abandoned at its present length in 1852. The present jetty was built in the early 1900s and is soon to be altered to take larger vessels.

La Maseline Harbour in Sark was started in 1939 but work was stopped during World War 2 and not restarted until 1946; it was finally completed in 1948 and replaced the much smaller Creux Harbour, which is now used only by yachts and fishing boats.

In looking at coasters in the Channel Islands, this book generally follows the route outlined above. After a selection of older monochrome images, we begin on the island of Jersey and then look at Guernsey's two ports followed by Alderney and Sark.

ACKNOWLEDGEMENTS

I owe a big debt of gratitude to all the photographers who have loaned material to me for this book who are credited individually below each photograph. Thanks also to Dr John Renouf for preparing the maps of each island and to Robert Le Maistre for his help with information, and to my wife Ann for helping with the proof reading etc. I also wish to record my thanks to Gil Mayes for his marvellous effort in ensuring the accuracy of details about the ships. Any errors that remain are my own responsibility. Finally I wish to offer my thanks to Bernard McCall for prompting me to produce this book, to the *Coastal Shipping* "crew" who have helped with production, and to the Amadeus Press who have brought the book to its ultimate conclusion.

Dave Hocquard   Jersey   December 2006

Published by Bernard McCall, 400 Nore Road, Portishead, Bristol, BS20 8EZ, England. Website : www.coastalshipping.co.uk
Telephone/fax : 01275 846178. E-mail : bernard@coastalshipping.co.uk
All distribution enquiries should be addressed to the publisher.

Printed by Amadeus Press, Ezra House, West 26 Business Park, Cleckheaton, West Yorkshire, BD19 4TQ
Telephone : 01274 863210; fax : 01274 863211; e-mail : info@amadeuspress.co.uk; website : www.amadeuspress.co.uk

ISBN : 978-1-902953-26-7

*Front cover : On a sunny day in October 1990, the **Port Soif** sets off from St Peter Port, the capital of Guernsey. More details of this ship will be found on page 80. She was owned by Captain Derick Goubert, a keen enthusiast as is evident from this book and also one of the last owner/masters to work in the coastal trades around the UK and near-continent.*

(Bernard McCall)

*Back cover : The bright sunny evening of 21 July 1975 saw two arrivals in St Helier Harbour. First is the Famagusta-registered **Galstar** (CYP, 498grt/57) from the North Wales port of Mostyn with a full cargo of fertiliser. Following her is the Danish **Lone Bres** (DNK, 499gt/62) from Kotka with sawn timber. Above the bow of the **Galstar** can be seen the beginnings of the breakwater for the present tanker berth, tidal marina and fish quay.*

(Dave Hocquard)

THE CHANNEL ISLANDS

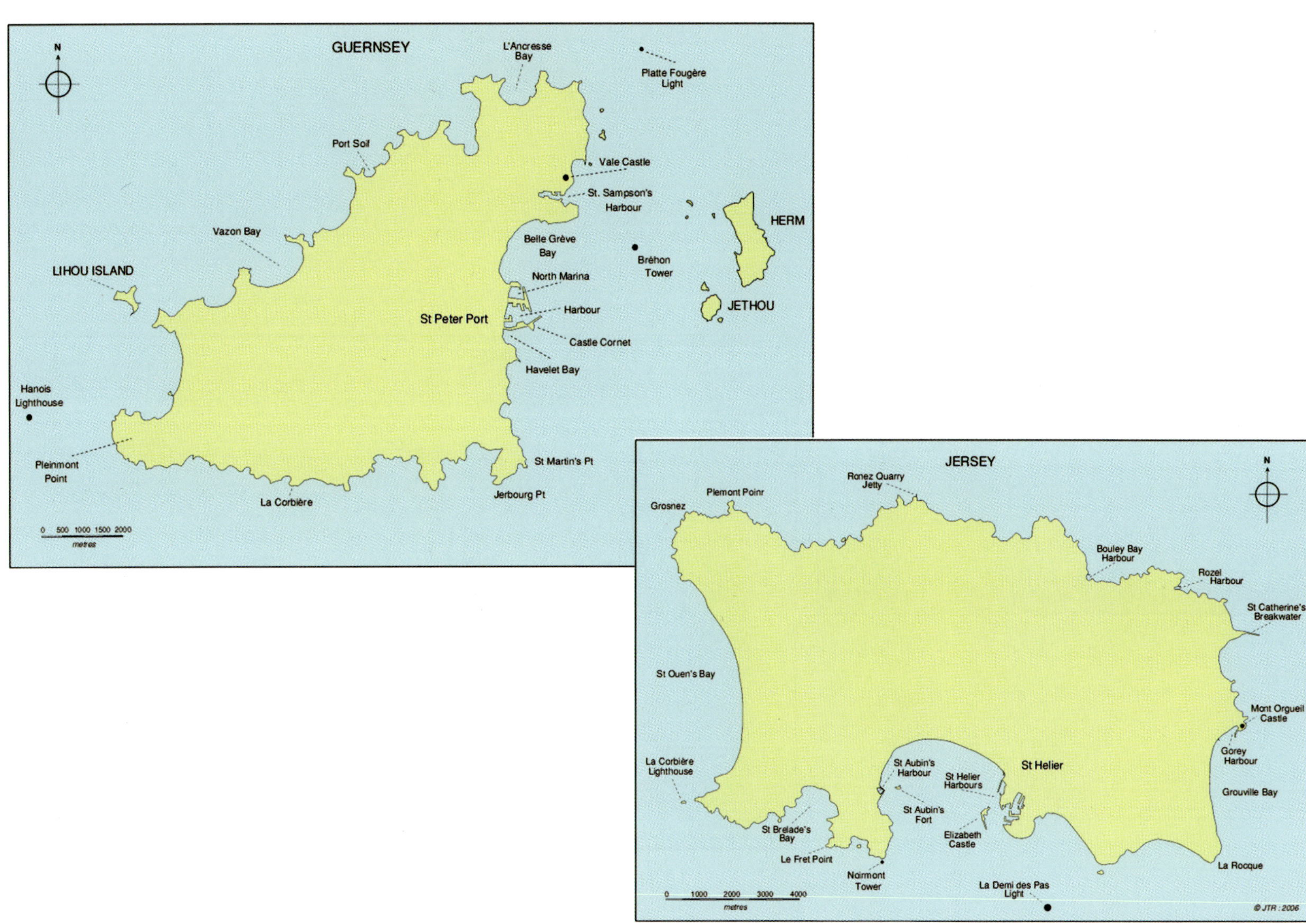

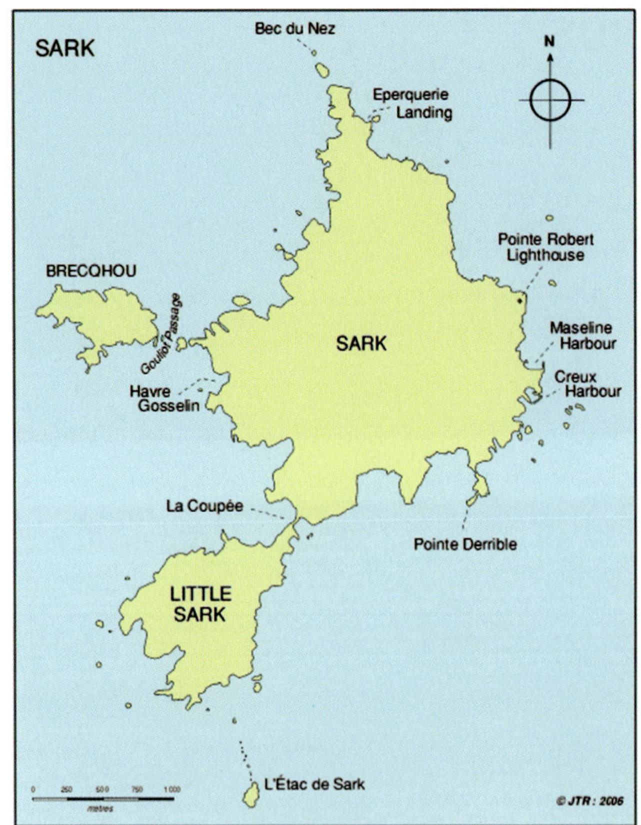
SARK
Bec du Nez
Eperquerie Landing
N
Pointe Robert Lighthouse
BRECQHOU
Goulot Passage
SARK
Maseline Harbour
Creux Harbour
Havre Gosselin
La Coupée
Pointe Derrible
LITTLE SARK
L'Étac de Sark
© JTR : 2006

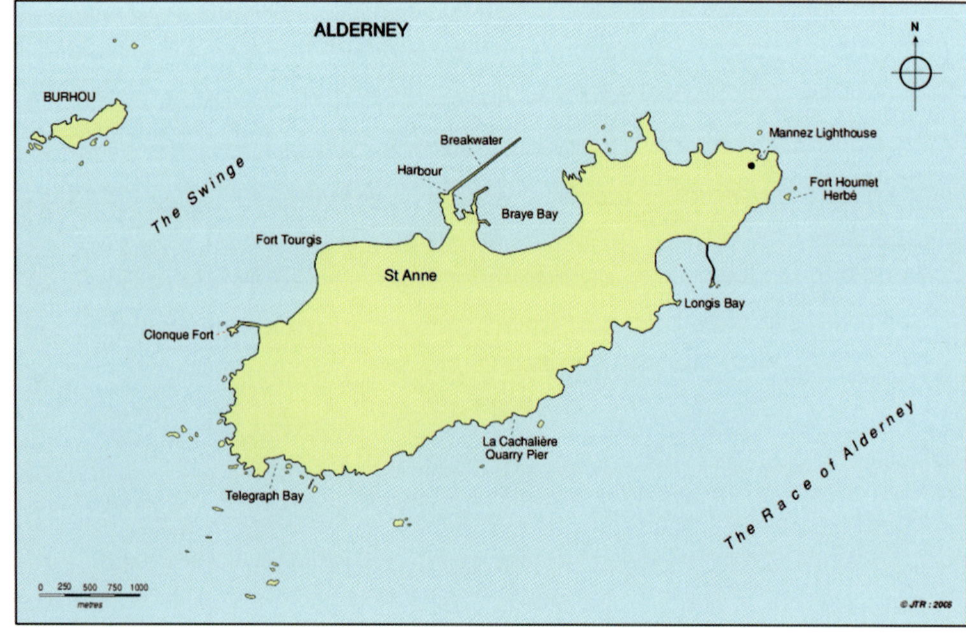
ALDERNEY
N
BURHOU
Breakwater
Mannez Lighthouse
Harbour
The Swinge
Fort Houmet Herbé
Braye Bay
Fort Tourgis
St Anne
Longis Bay
Clonque Fort
La Cachalière Quarry Pier
Telegraph Bay
The Race of Alderney
0 250 500 750 1000
metres
© JTR : 2006

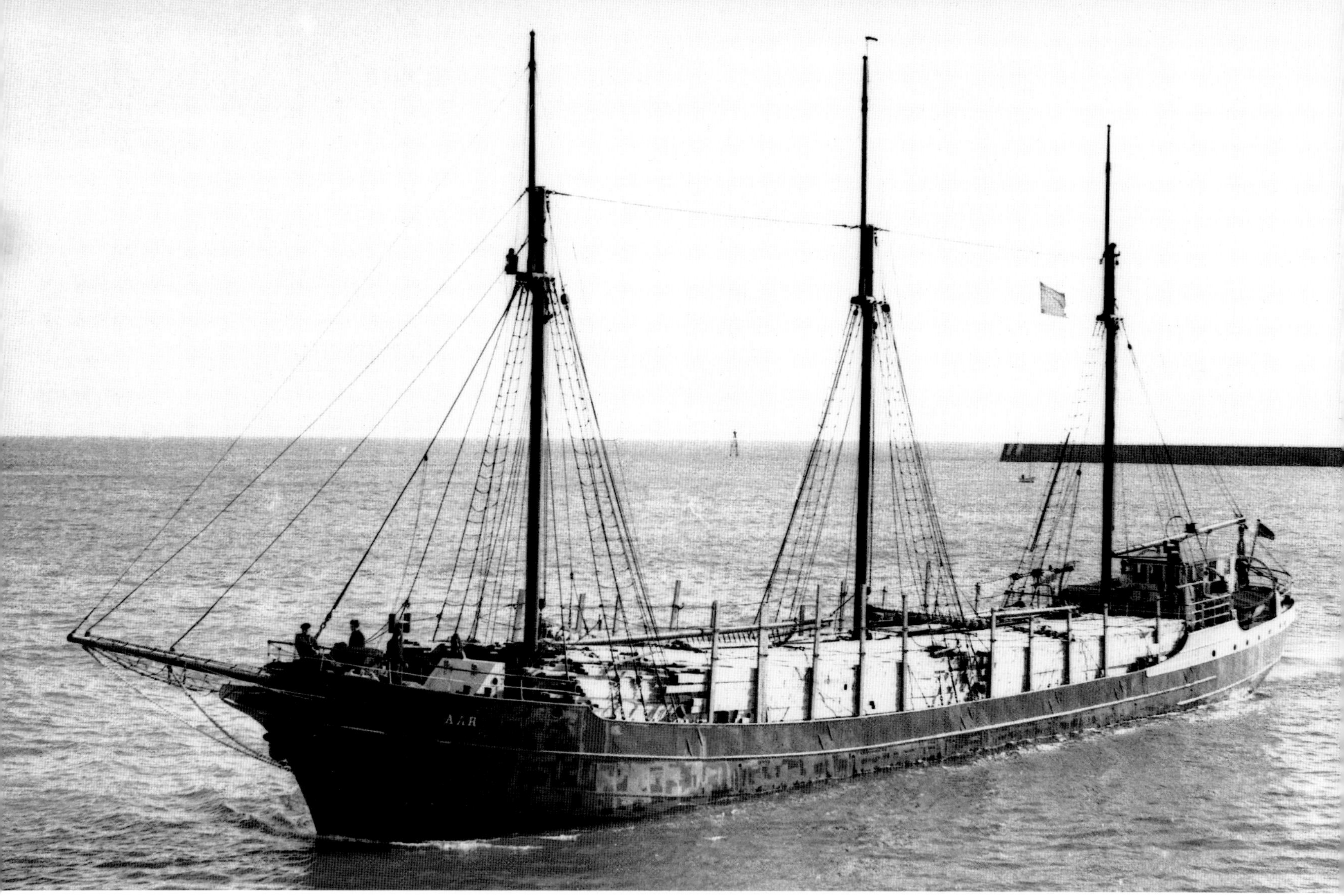

Here is the rare sight of a 3-masted schooner entering harbour in the evening sunshine of 8 May 1955 taken from the end of St Helier's Albert Pier, the best vantage point from late afternoon. In the background is Elizabeth Castle breakwater which protects the harbour entrance from the south-westerly Atlantic swells. The ***Aar*** (DEU, 330grt/32) arrives from Turku/Åbo with timber. She was one of the many small motorised schooners built by C Lühring at Hammelwarden and she had been lengthened twice, firstly in 1938 and later in 1952. She was sold out of commercial service in 1973 to be converted into a charter yacht.

(Dave Hocquard)

Having dropped her starboard anchor, turned around and put ashore bow and stern lines, the ***Pentland Firth*** (GBR, 594grt/55) owned by Northern Coasters Ltd (G T Gillie & Blair Ltd, managers) of Newcastle, prepares to go astern to load stone at Ronez Quarry's jetty on the north coast of Jersey in the morning sunshine of 16 September 1956. Loading would take approximately two hours using a gravity feed shoot, with the ship having to be winched backwards and forwards to trim the cargo. When loading was complete, all lines would be let go. Once clear of the land, hatches would be covered and derricks stowed. After a period of stormy weather, as many as four ships could be loaded in a day.

(Dave Hocquard)

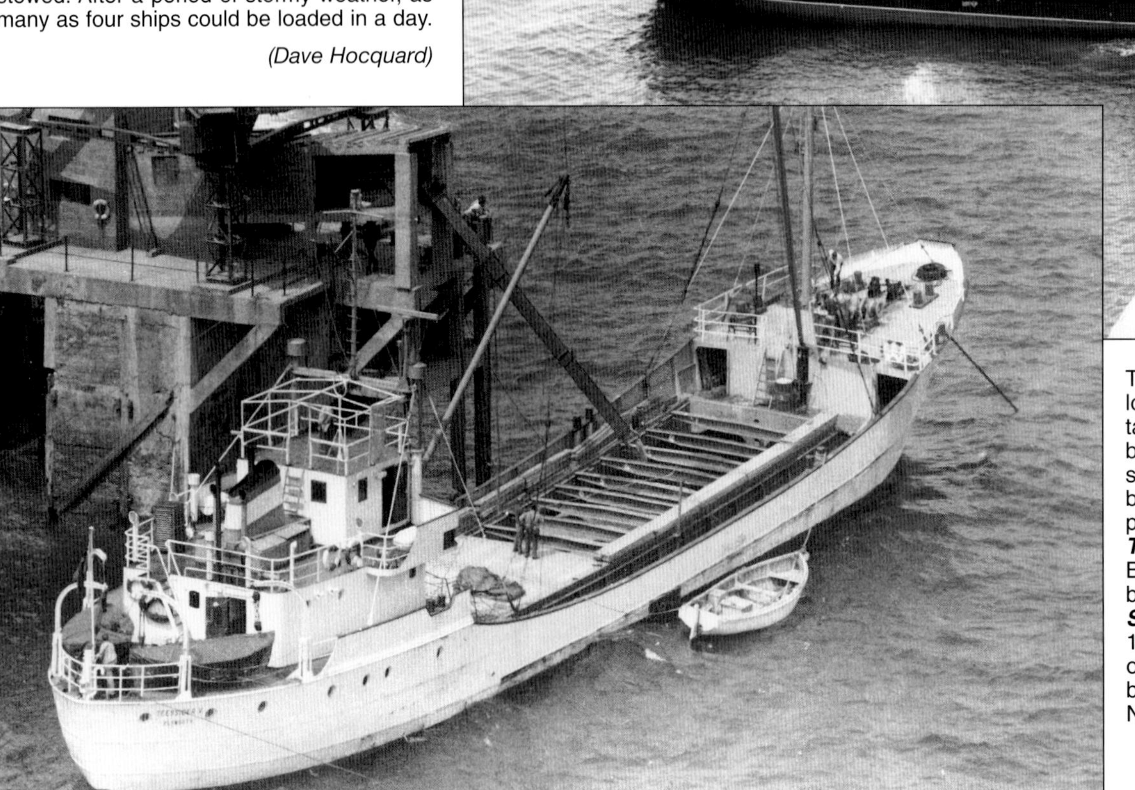

This view of the ***Teessider V*** (GBR, 399grt/55) loading stone at Ronez Quarry's Jetty was taken from the cliff top coastal road and gives a better idea of the loading gear. The end of the shute is held in place by the Scotch derrick the base of which can be seen in the top left of the photograph. Registered in Plymouth, the ***Teessider V*** was owned by Blakecrest Ltd, Barking, when the photo was taken. She was built at the Claus Lühring shipyard in Brake as ***Stadland*** and came into British ownership in 1971. Five years later, she was sold to Greek owners and renamed ***Aghia Anargyri*** in 1977, becoming ***Arvi*** in 1983 and then ***Paraiso***. Nothing has been heard of her since 2001.

(Dave Hocquard)

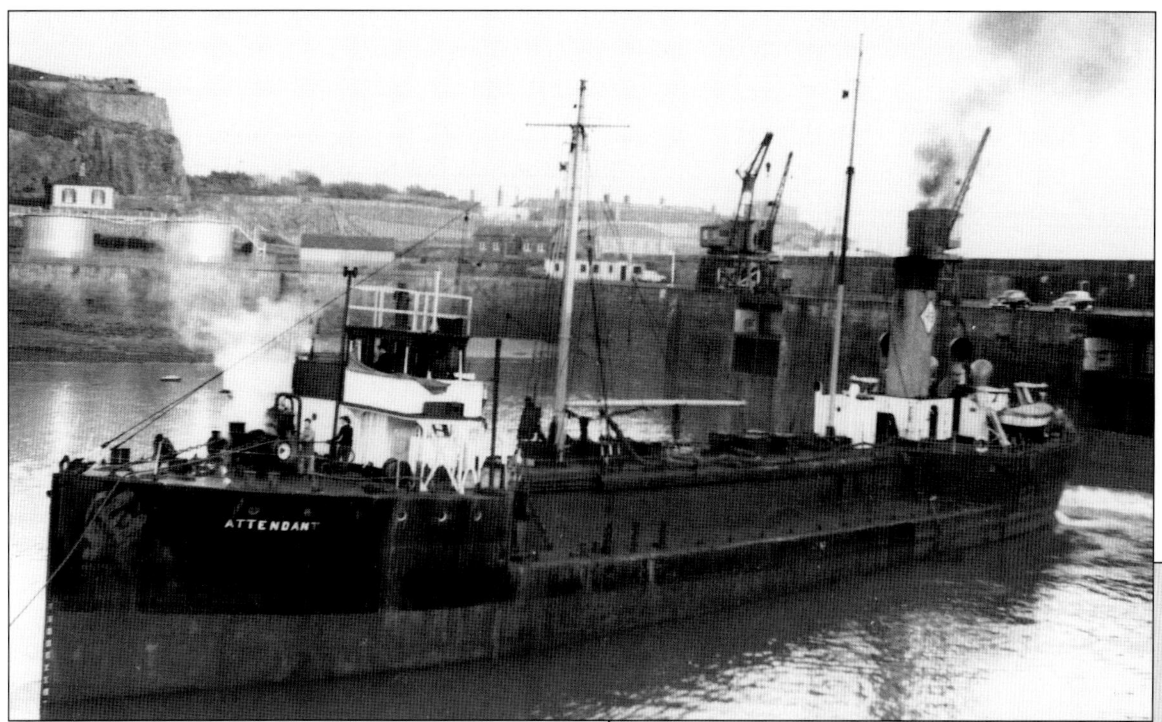

With an unusual profile more akin to a Canadian Great Lakes steamer, the ***Attendant*** (GBR, 999grt/14) has discharged her cargo of gas oil for Jersey's electricity power station at the East Cross berth on St Helier's Victoria Pier prior to sailing during the afternoon of 15 February 1959 for Alderney to discharge the remainder of her cargo. Built by Chatham dockyard, the ***Attendant*** was the first of a large group of small tankers built during World War 1 by various British shipbuilders. Mostly sold to commercial owners after the end of hostilities, a few remained with the Admiralty on bunkering duties into the 1950s. Owned by Hemsley Bell Ltd of Southampton, she survived until October 1964 when she was broken up by Lacmots Ltd at Queenborough.

(Dave Hocquard)

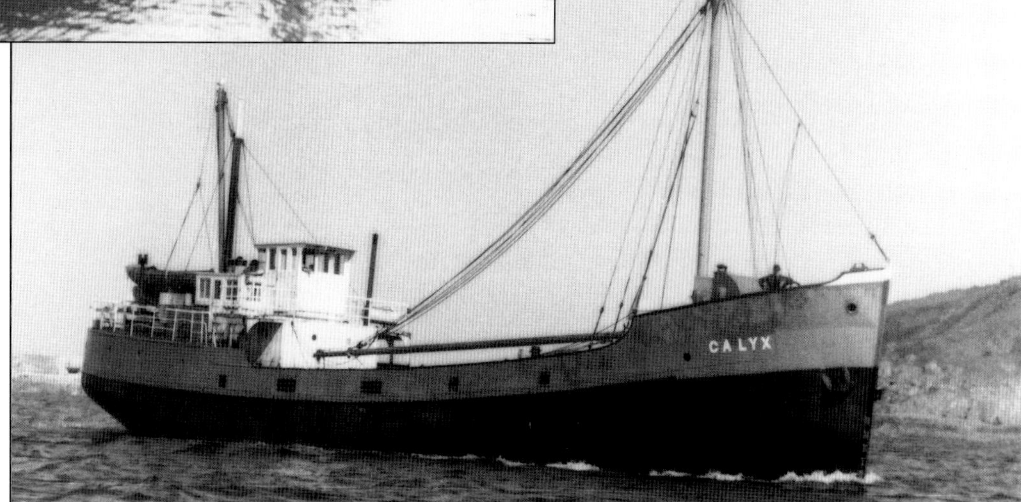

Having just rounded the breakwater and heading towards Braye Harbour, Alderney, in 1964 while on charter to Commodore Shipping and carrying cauliflowers to Portsmouth, the ***Calyx*** (GBR, 212grt/29) was owned at the time by Peter Herbert's Herb Ship Ltd, Bude. Having bought her as a constructive total loss at Fishguard where she had been damaged in a gale during February 1963, Captain Herbert had just spent some time refitting the ***Calyx*** in the Richmond Dry Dock at Appledore. She was sold on to other UK owners in July 1964 and was then fitted with a new engine and underwent further modifications and refurbishment. There were several other changes of ownership until she sank near the dock at Ipswich on 21 March 1973. She was later refloated and broken up in Ipswich dock.

(the late Peter Herbert)

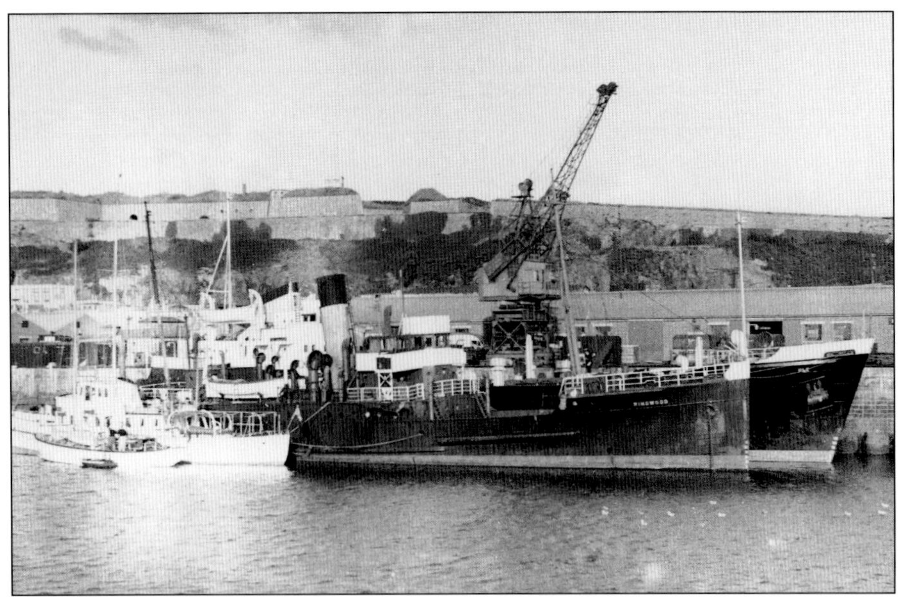

The old and new together at the New North Quay's berth 7 in St Helier. On the inside is British Rail's new cargo vessel ***Elk*** (GBR, 745grt/59) on one of her first sailings to Jersey with the rundown-looking steamer ***Ringwood*** (GBR, 755grt/26). This vessel was one of nine similar cargo vessels built for the Southern Railway in the 1920s and, seen on 29 August 1959, she was on one of her last sailings prior to being sold to shipbreakers in Holland before the end of the year. The ***Elk*** passed to Greek owners in 1972 and was converted into a ro/ro vehicle ferry. Her end came on 12 February 1976 when she sank north of Giannutri Island during a voyage from Leghorn to Alexandria.

(Dave Hocquard)

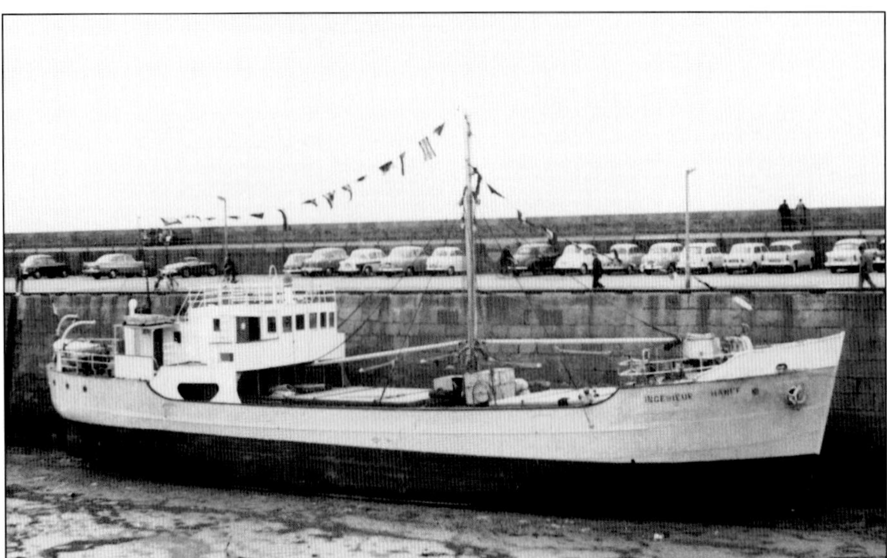

Seen here on a lay-by berth at the top of the Albert Pier in St Helier, the small French coaster ***Ingénieur en Chef Hanff*** (199grt/32) was dressed overall for a Royal visitor on 11 May 1963. She had arrived from the small Breton port of Dalhouet with a cargo of grain in bulk and sailed for Poole in ballast three days later. She began life as the cable ship ***Poolster*** for the Dutch Government and was taken over by Germany in 1940, being passed to the French Government in 1945. She was converted to a dry cargo coaster in 1949 on sale to A P Nagel, of Brest.

(Dave Hocquard)

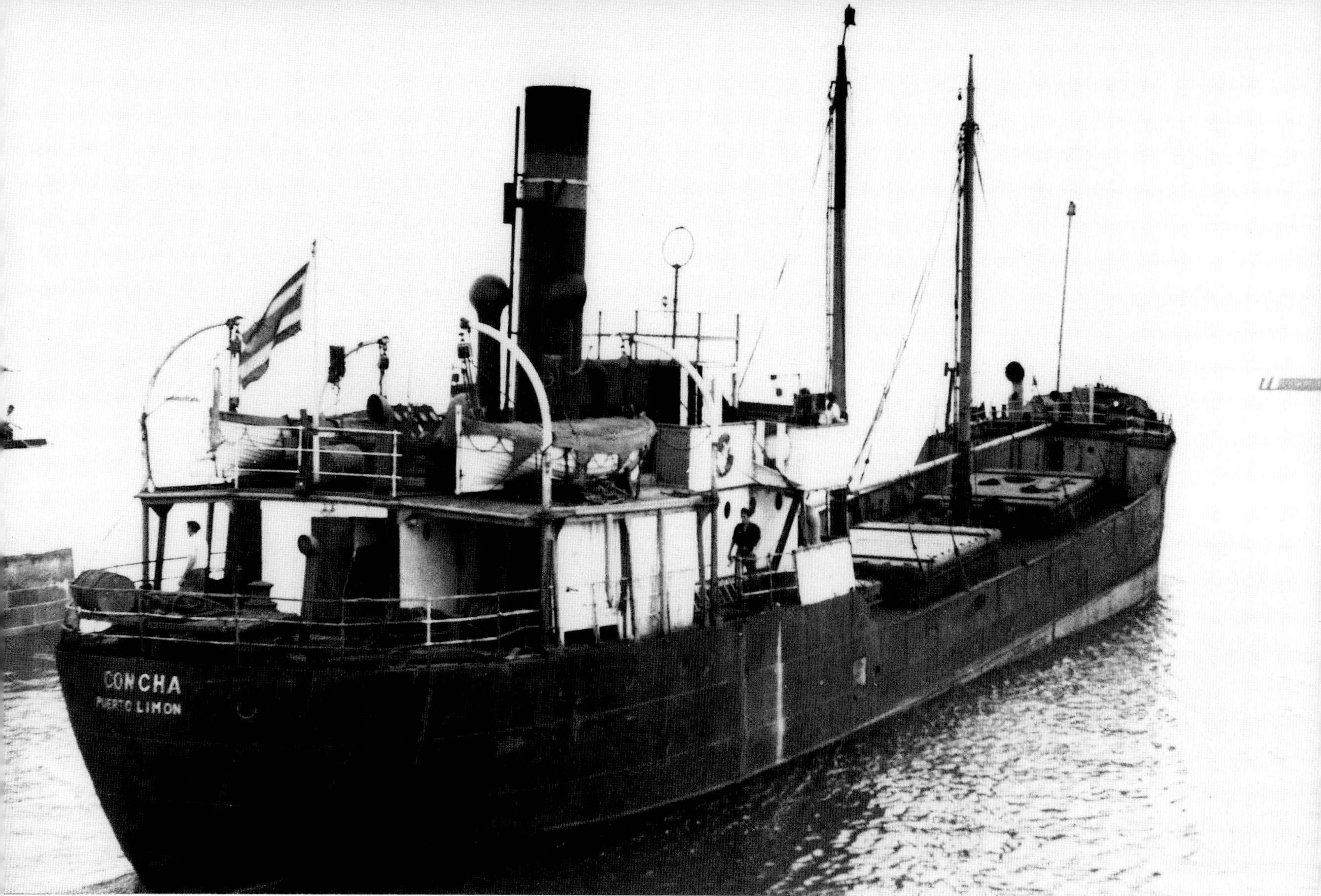

The first and only Costa Rican flag coaster to visit St Helier Harbour to the author's knowledge was the ***Concha*** (662grt/19) - she was also possibly the most decrepit. Having arriving in ballast from Nantes on 19 July 1958, she loaded spent oxide before sailing the same day for Poole. Originally Swedish owned, she passed to London owners in 1953 as ***Mairoula M*** and became ***Concha*** in 1956. Despite the Costa Rican flag, she was still owned in London. She sank in the Irish Sea following fire and explosion in her engine room on 10 September 1958.

(Dave Hocquard)

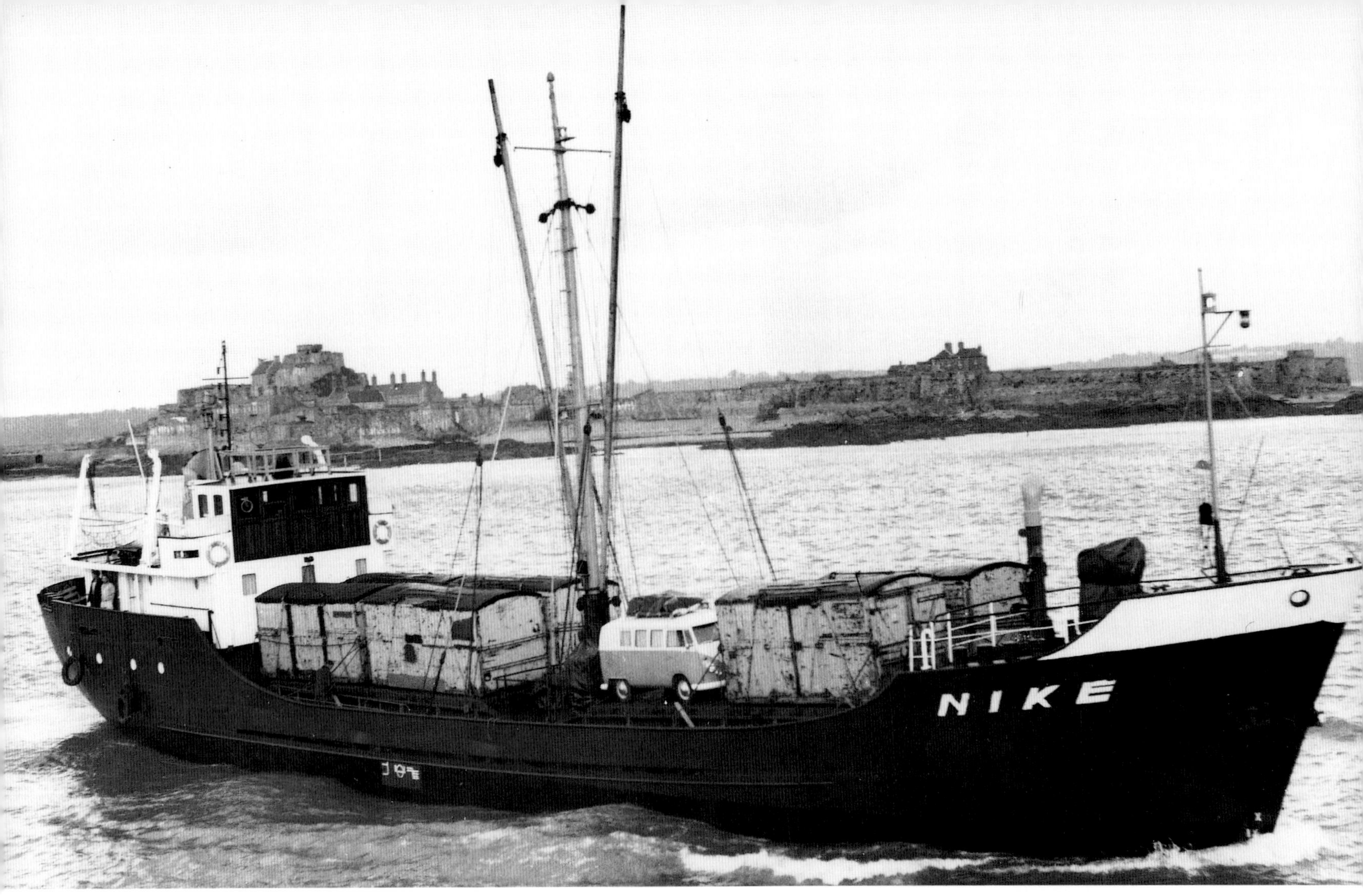

Typical of the many small Dutch owned and built coasters that traded to the islands in the 1950s is the ***Nike*** (NLD, 367grt/57) seen here while on long term charter to Commodore Shipping Co Ltd, of Guernsey, and painted in this company's colours. She is arriving at St Helier on 5 July 1967 from St Peter Port, Guernsey, with a deck cargo of cars and former British Rail containers which brought Commodore into the container age. The 15th century Elizabeth Castle makes an interesting backdrop to photographs taken from the outside corner of the Victoria Pierhead and is best seen from early morning to early afternoon.

(Dave Hocquard)

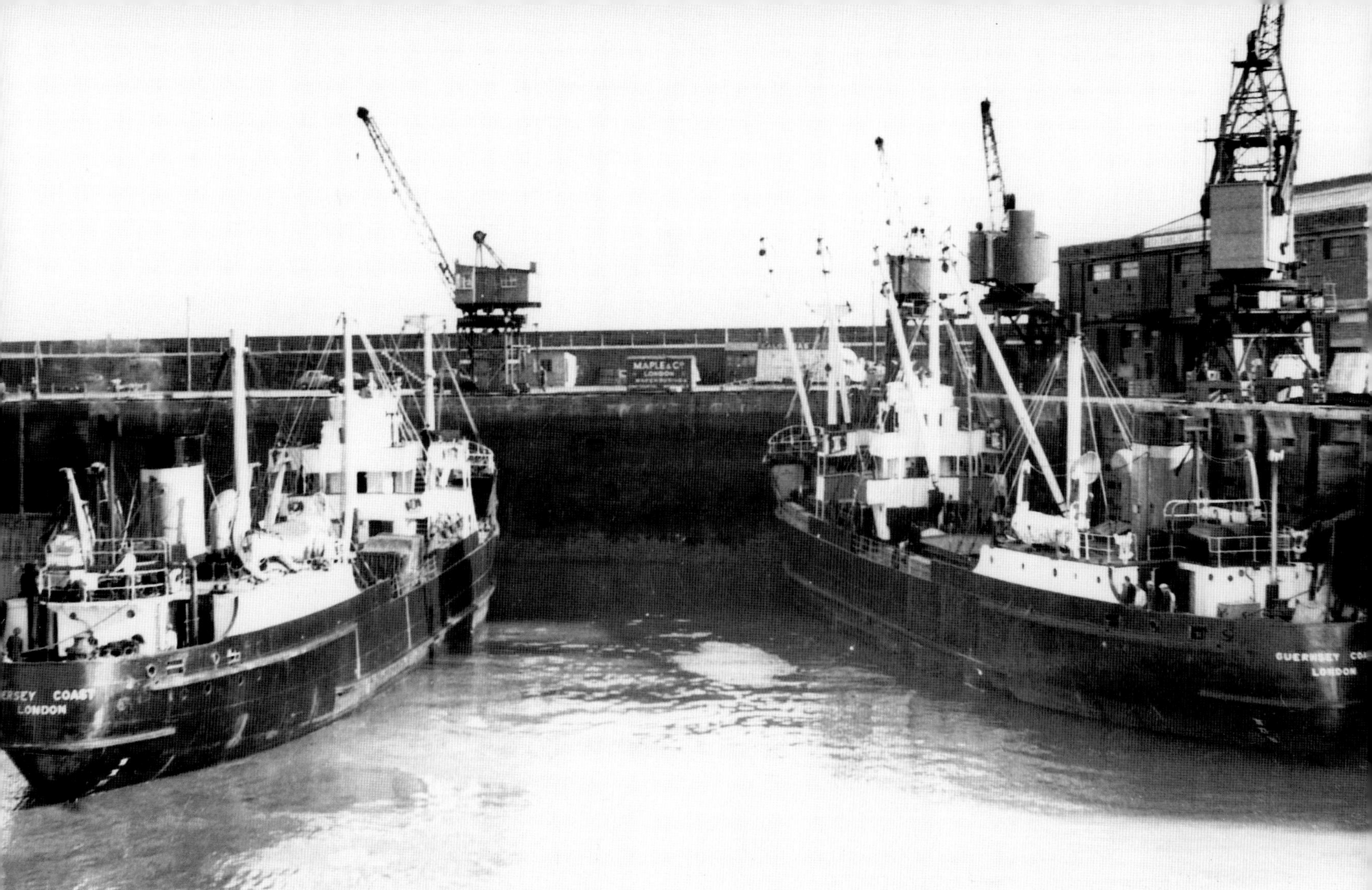

A rare scene which finds two sisterships, the ***Jersey Coast*** (GBR, 687grt/40) and ***Guernsey Coast*** (GBR, 646grt/38) of the British Channel Islands Shipping Co Ltd, of London, in St Helier Harbour together in the evening sunlight of 15 July 1958. The ***Jersey Coast*** is just pulling away from the west cross-berth on the Victoria Pier and bound for Guernsey. The ***Guernsey Coast*** is discharging general cargo in the London Boat berth normally used by the B. C. I. S. ships. The former ship was sold to Saudi Arabian owners in late 1967. The latter had the misfortune to have sunk in mid English Channel after colliding with the ***Catcher*** (LBR, 7238grt/44) during a voyage from St Peter Port to Shoreham with a cargo of tomatoes on 8 August 1964.

(Dave Hocquard)

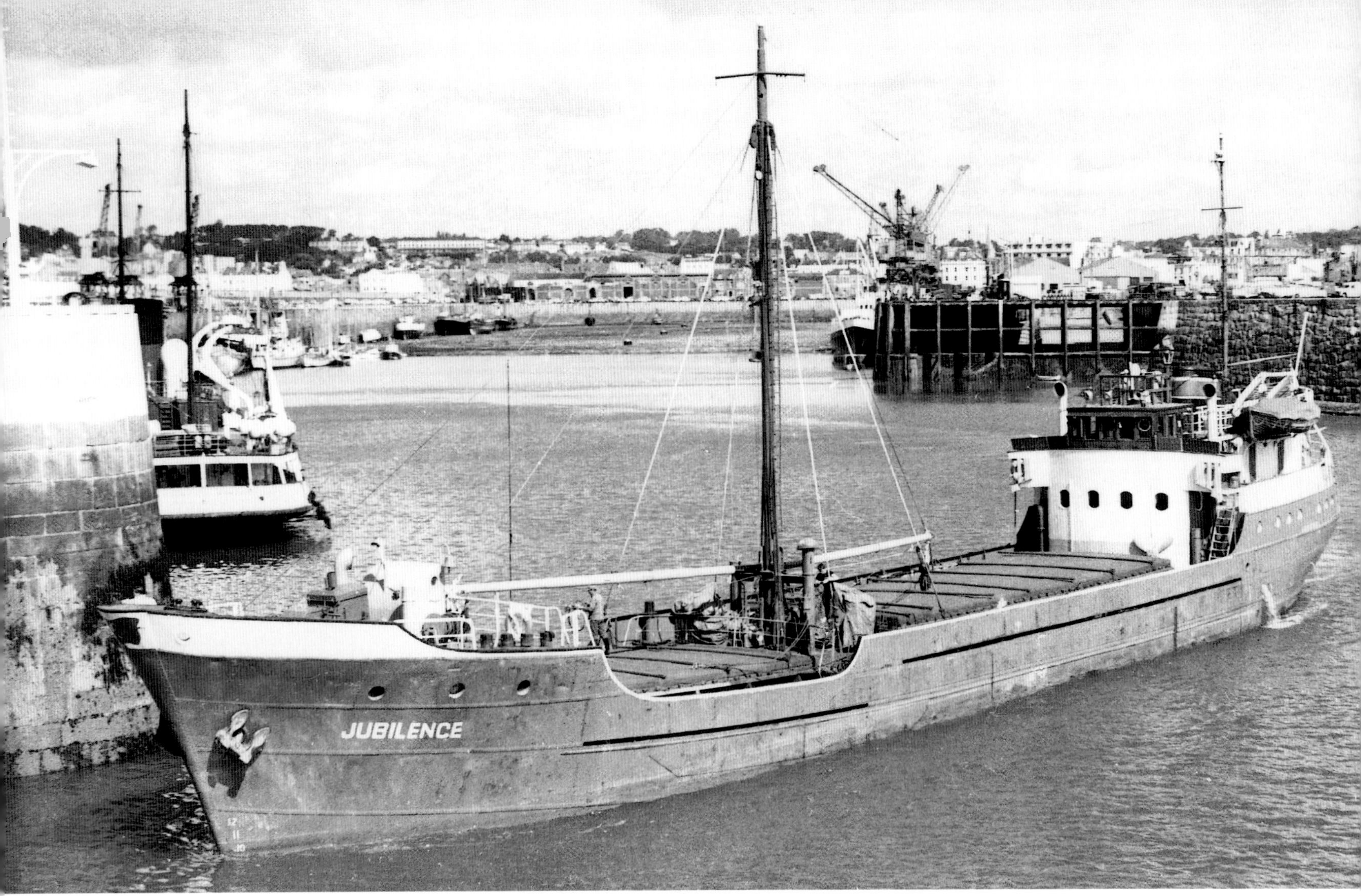

This view of the ***Jubilence*** (GBR, 591grt/50) sailing from St Helier Harbour on 9 September 1965 was taken from the inside of the Victoria Pier head and gives a good idea of the layout of the main harbour before the advent of the yacht marina. In the background can be seen the cross wall and the drying out area known as the Bank, with lay-by berths on the left hand side. The slipway and landing stage on the end of the New North Quay were originally built for the Great Western Railway mail steamers in the 1890s. The ***Jubilence*** was bound for Portsmouth with a cargo of coke breeze from the gas works.

(Dave Hocquard)

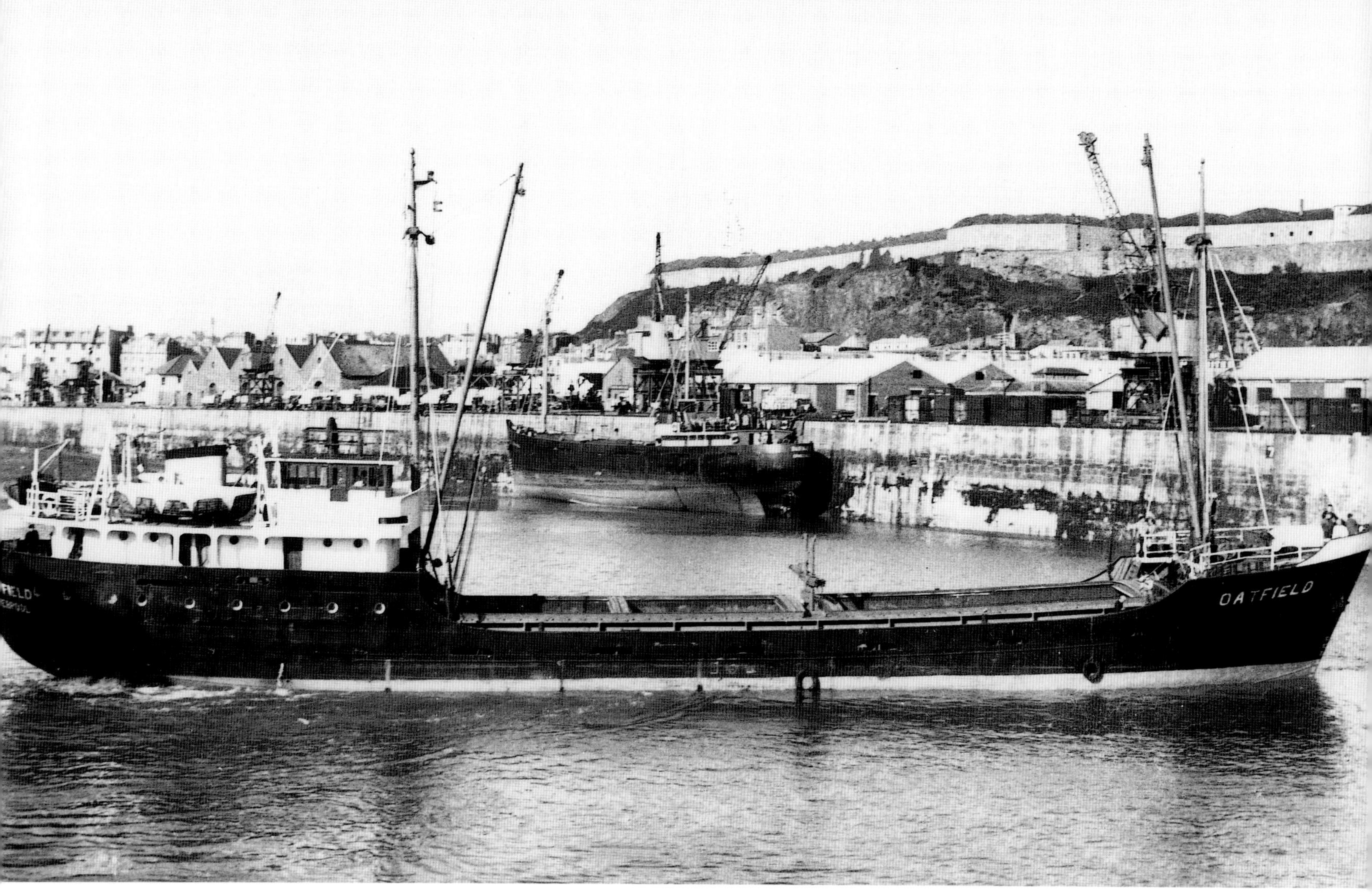

A classic scene of St Helier Harbour taken on 10 June 1955 with the Zillah Shipping Co's ***Oatfield*** (GBR, 538grt/52) outward bound for Liverpool having loaded 417 tons of Jersey Royal potatoes. In the background is George Gibson's ***Durward*** (GBR, 419grt/40) loading potatoes for Newcastle with a queue of lorries carrying potatoes still to be loaded; she sailed in the late evening with 497 tons. Like most coasters of their generation, both vessels still had derricks and no steel hatch covers, no radar and no autopilot. There are a few of British Rail's old wooden containers on the quayside.

(Dave Hocquard)

Seen approaching berth 4 on St Helier's Albert Pier on the top of a big autumnal spring tide on 27 September 1964 is the steel-built auxiliary 2-masted schooner ***Result*** (GBR, 125grt/1893). She was to discharge her cargo of 160 tons of bagged lime brought from Littlehampton. A survivor from a bygone age, she worked on until the 1970s. She was then sold to the Ulster Folk Museum near Belfast and lifted ashore and taken to the museum by road where she remains to this day. There have been reports that she will be restored to sailing condition. Loading at berth 3 is British Rail's mail vessel ***Caesarea*** (GBR, 4174grt/60) which will later sail at 0800 to St Peter Port and Weymouth.

(Dave Hocquard)

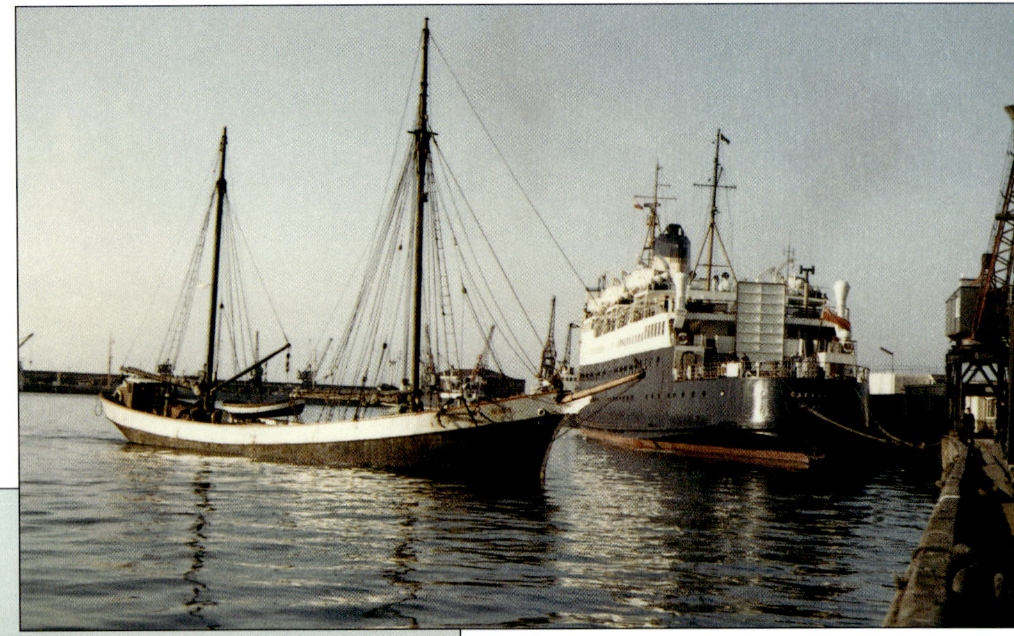

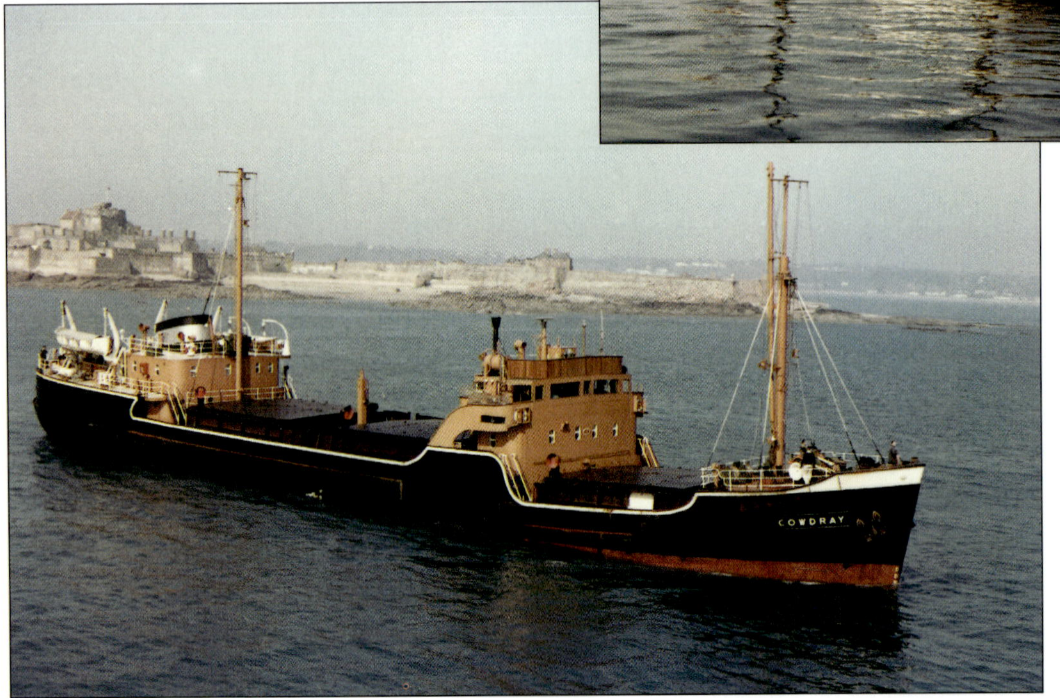

On the sunny spring morning of 26 April 1964 with the backdrop of the medieval Elizabeth Castle, Stephenson Clarke's fine motor collier ***Cowdray*** (GBR, 1748grt/59), a product of Burntisland Shipbuilding Co Ltd, arrives with the fortnightly cargo of around 2,000 tons of gas coal from Goole. She was sold to J Kelly Ltd in 1976 and was renamed ***Ballycastle***. She was purchased by Lebanese owners in 1981 and was renamed ***Aref***, eventually being broken up at Eleusis in September 1986.

(Dave Hocquard)

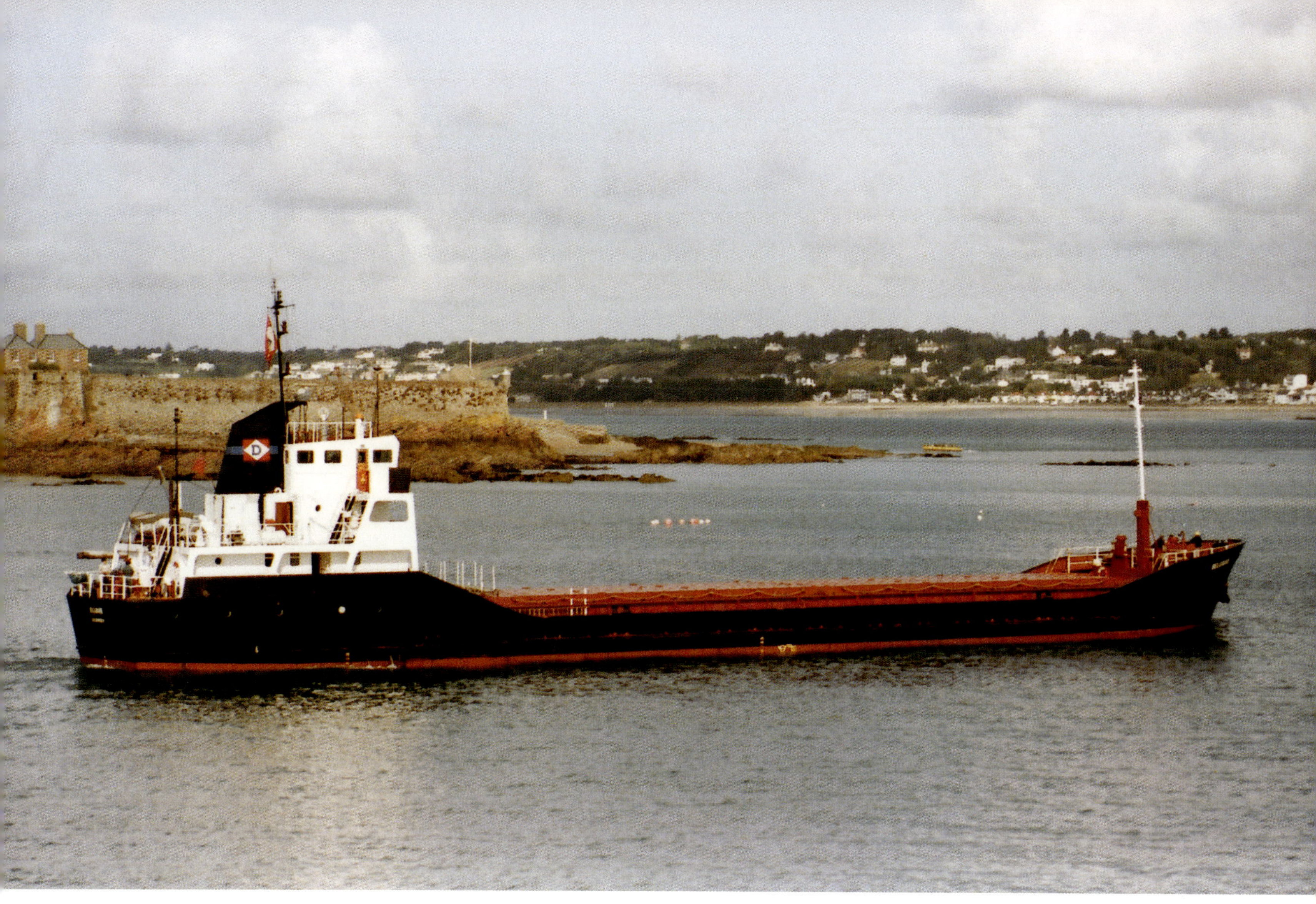

A very smart ***Belgrave*** (GBR, 985grt/78) arrives at St Helier Harbour on a sunny autumn day, 3 October 1982, with a full cargo of house coal. She was one of three identical bulk cargo coasters built for Onesimus Dorey by James W Cook & Co Ltd at Wivenhoe (Essex) in the late 1970s. The company and all three ships were sold to James Fisher in 1986 and the ships were soon chartered out. After serving a number of other owners she met her end on 14 February 2005 when she sank north of Crete while bound from Istanbul to Misurata with containers.

(Dave Hocquard)

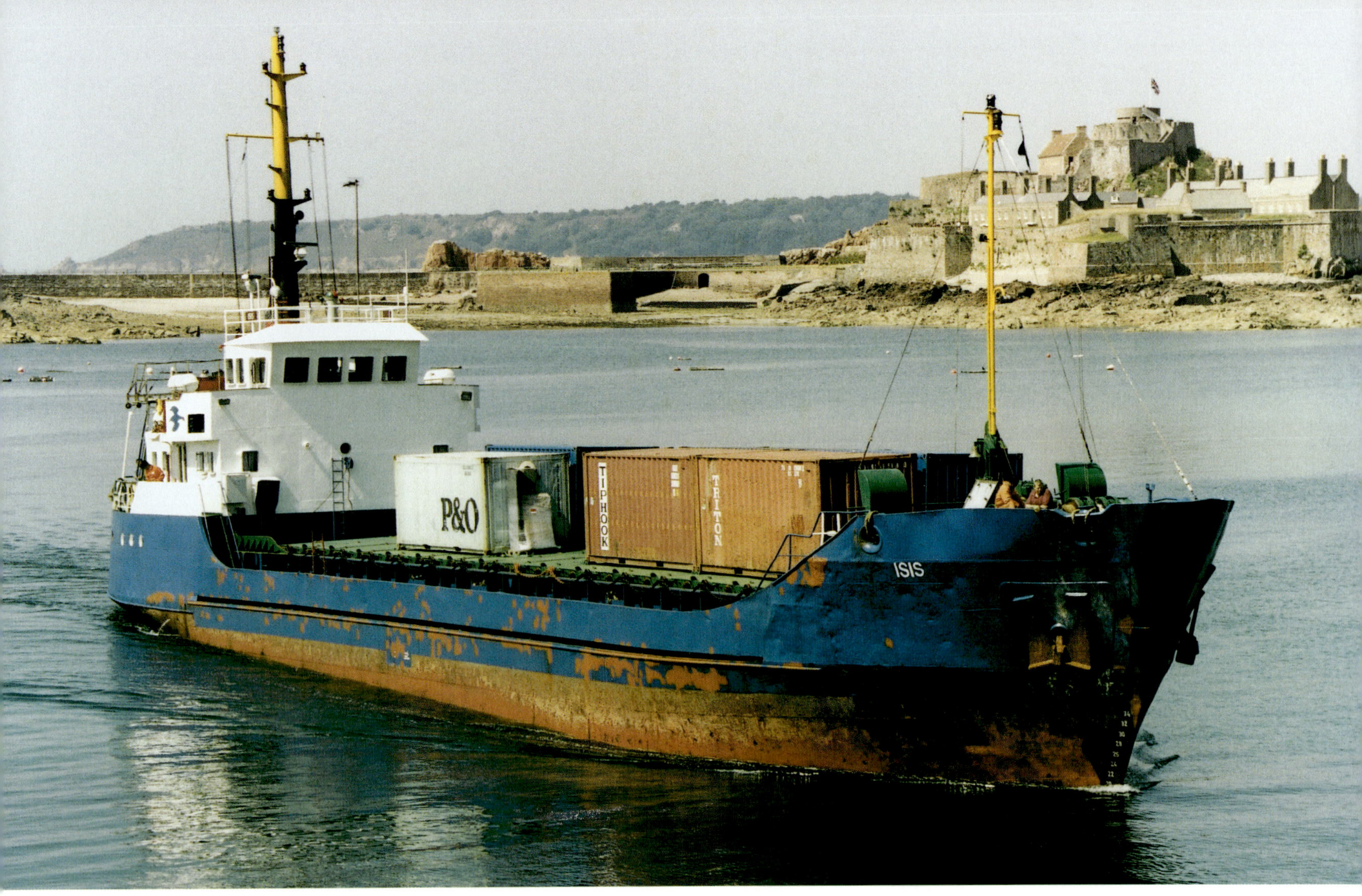

On warm sunny 28 July 2004, the ***Isis*** (IOM, 674gt/78) approaches St Helier pierheads from Portland with containers and would sail in a few hours for Ridderhaven inland from Rotterdam. Built by Jadewerft at Wilhelmshaven, the ***Isis*** began life as Shamrock Shipping's ***David Dorman*** and was originally used in the coal trade. Between May 1989 and May 1994, she traded for Dennison Shipping as ***Deer Sound***. Since entering the fleet of Alderney Shipping, she has been used as a container ship (24 TEU) along with her sistership ***Burhou I*** (the I being an abbreviation for island), formerly the ***Edgar Dorman***.

(Dave Hocquard)

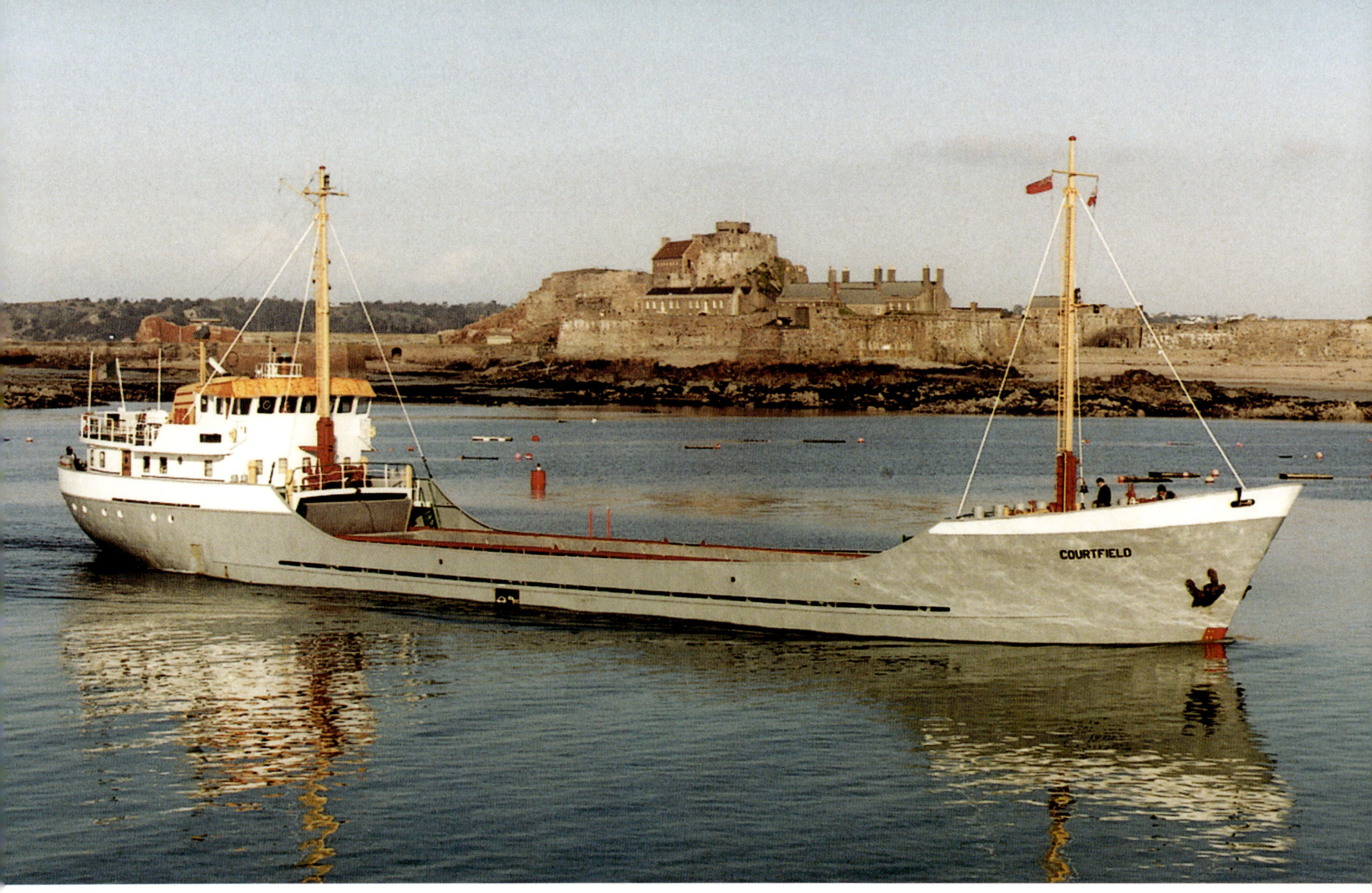

This scene of Harris & Dixon's ***Courtfield*** (IRL, 500grt/68) moving gracefully up to the harbour mouth at St Helier on 23 April 1991 is, to my mind, as near to perfection as possible, even bearing in mind that she is a well-painted ship. She is arriving from Plymouth with a cargo of sand. The ***Courtfield*** was well travelled. Built at the Scheepswerf "Voorwaarts" yard in Martenshoek as ***Constance***, she crossed the Atlantic Ocean to Canada. 1977 saw her in the Arklow fleet as ***Arklow Bridge***. In 1981 she joined Carisbrooke Shipping as ***Mark-C*** until 1986. In 1991 she was sold to Ocean Research & Recovery Ltd, with Turks & Caicos Islands registry, and again crossed the Atlantic several times on charter to the U.S. Government. After several more renamings, she sank in the Caribbean in March 1997.

(Robert Le Maistre)

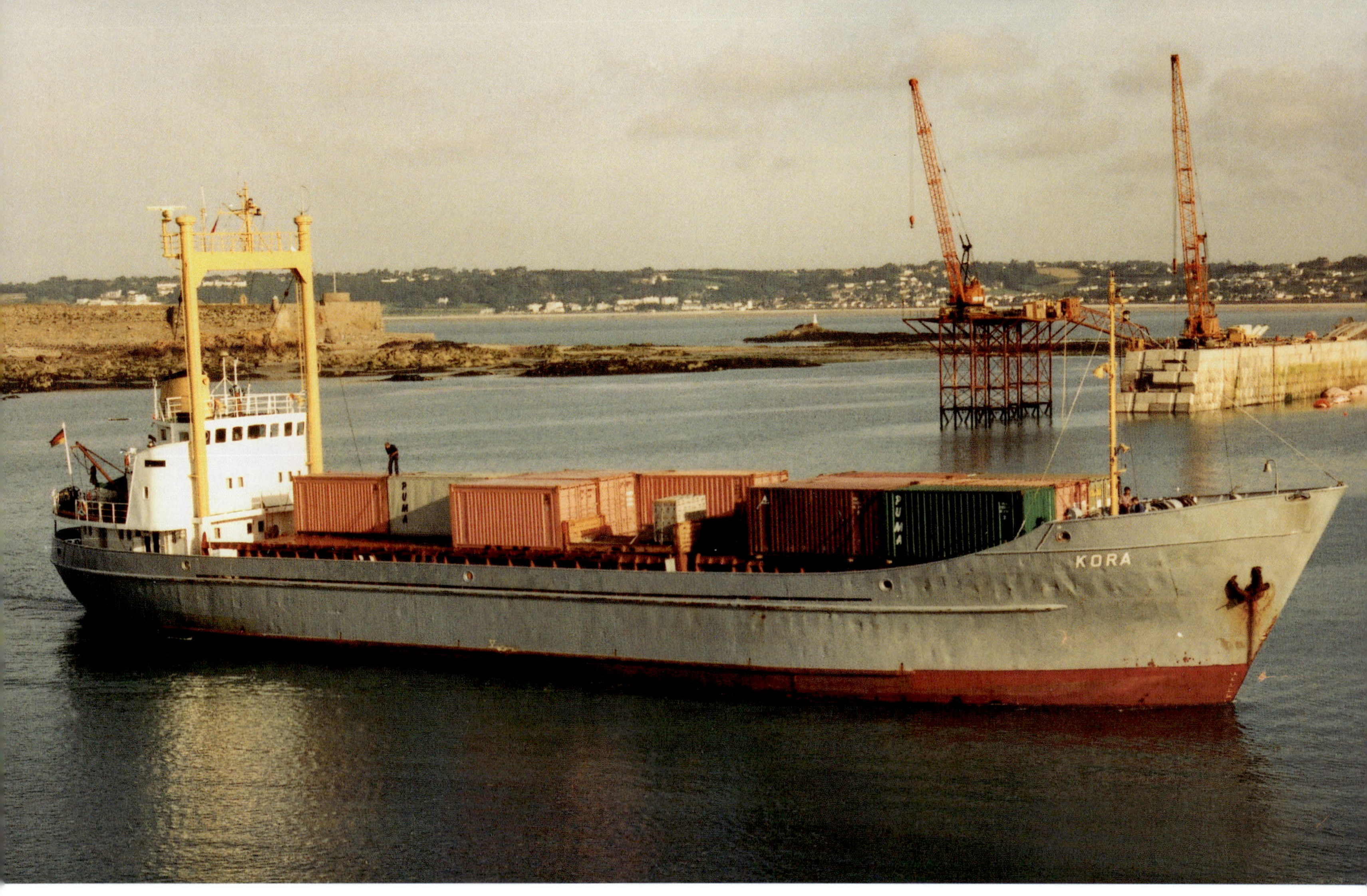

Type 33 container vessels from the J J Sietas shipyard on the outskirts of Hamburg were the ideal size to promote the container revolution to the Channel Islands. The ***Kora*** (DEU, 499grt/67) was one of many and the longest to serve the islands, having been on charter firstly to British Rail carrying tomatoes and cars between St Peter Port and Weymouth. Commodore employed her on most of their routes as needed. It was on Stork Lines' Rotterdam - Channel Islands route that she was to see her longest period of service from November 1985 to November 1993. She then passed to Caribbean owners for service out of Tampa (Florida) as ***Mylinda*** then ***Caytrans Caribe*** until 27 May 1998 when she sank after springing a leak four days previously.

(Dave Hocquard)

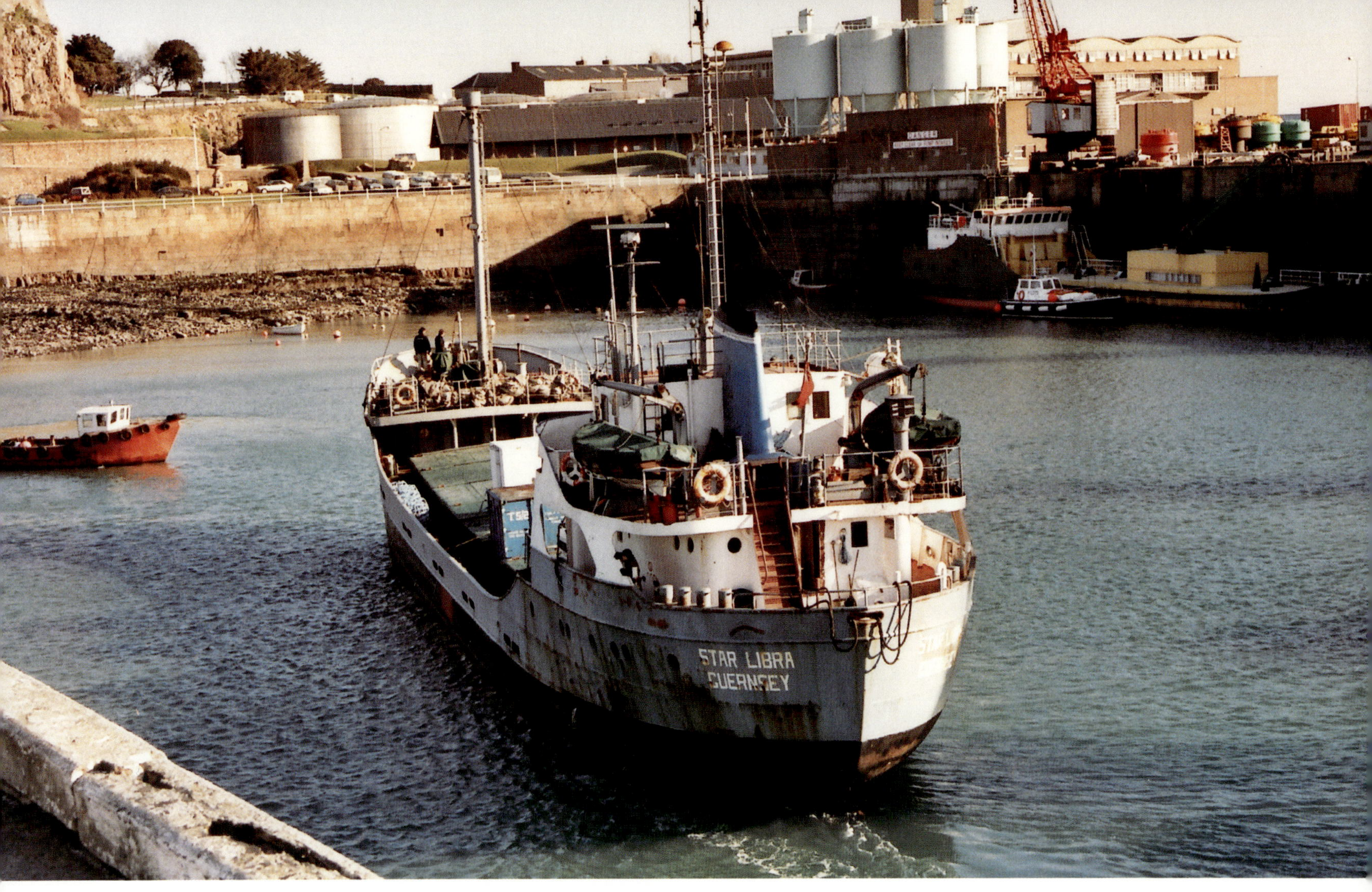

Having just arrived from Torquay with general cargo, the Guernsey-registered ***Star Libra*** (GBR, 429grt/58) of Torbay Seaways turns just inside the harbour mouth to berth on the Victoria Pier ahead of the cement carrier ***Ronez*** (GBR, 870grt/82) which was discharging bulk cement into the silos above her stern. Behind these is the island's electricity power station built in the late 1960s and dominating this part of the harbour. The ***Star Libra*** was an early Sietas standard-type single deck coaster and of a class distinguished by the designation Type 1, she was launched as ***Ernst De Buhr***, becoming ***August van Allworden*** in 1965 and ***Hohensee*** in 1982 and then ***Star Libra*** in 1985. She served Torbay Seaways for just five years before being sold and renamed ***Vasant***. Later changes of identity saw her become ***Crystal V*** in 1991, ***Kati K*** in 1995 and ***Rika*** in 2002.

(Dave Hocquard)

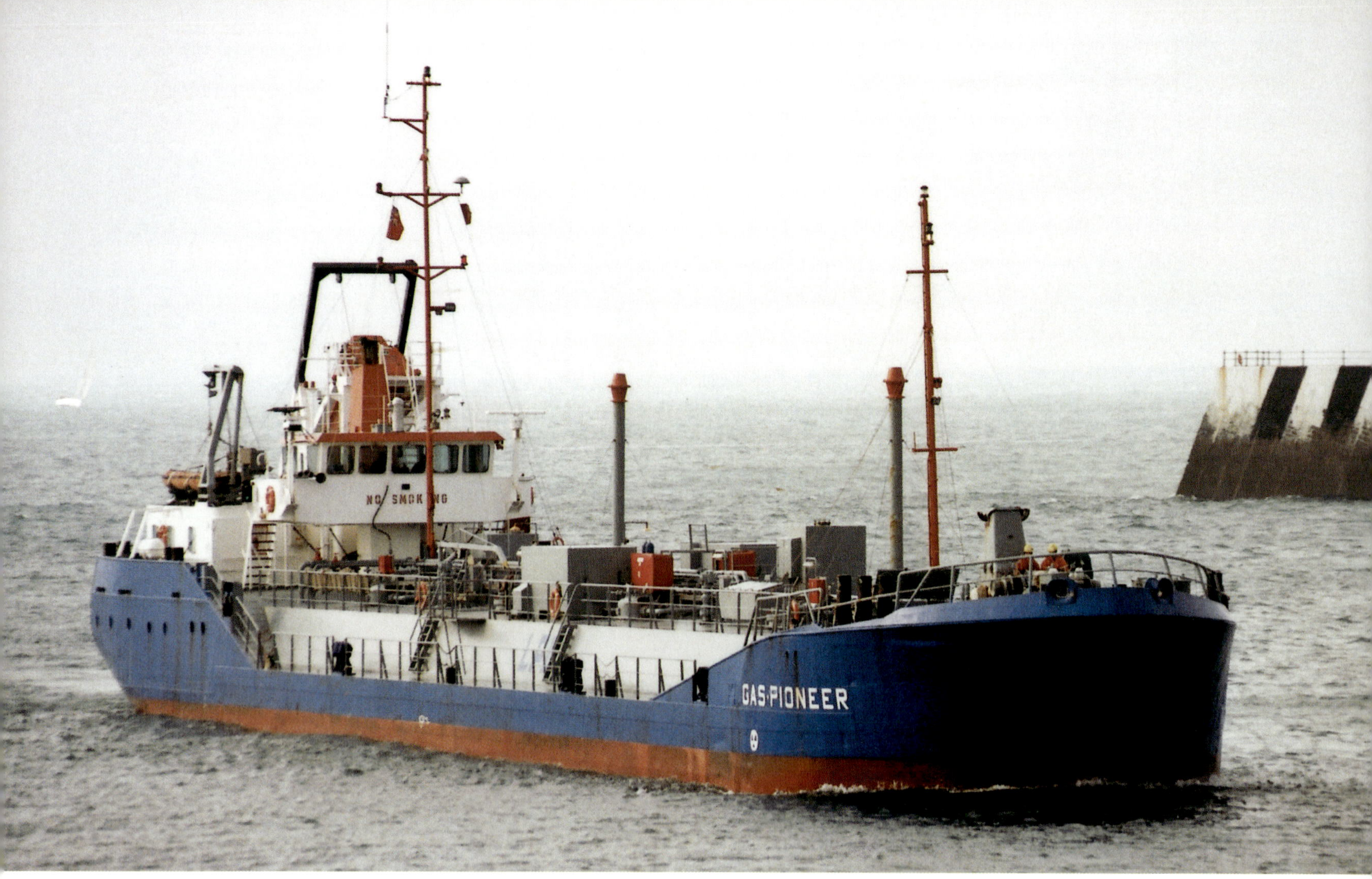

As will be seen on the next page, and also on the Guernsey pages, the import of liquefied petroleum gas (lpg) to the Channel Islands is an important trade. The ***Gas Pioneer*** (IOM, 1173gt/92) is not a regular caller for she usually trades across the Irish Sea from Milford Haven. However, on 25 February 2005, she is seen approaching St Helier with a part cargo from the Esso refinery at Fawley on Southampton Water, the balance of her cargo having already been discharged at St Sampson's in Guernsey. Surprisingly for a modern vessel, there is uncertainty about her early history. She was built at the Alblas shipyard in Hendrik-Ido-Ambacht and although most sources give 1992 as her year of construction, *Lloyd's Register* notes that she was converted from a non-propelled tank barge named ***Annagas I*** and this may have been between 1987 and 1992.

(Dave Hocquard)

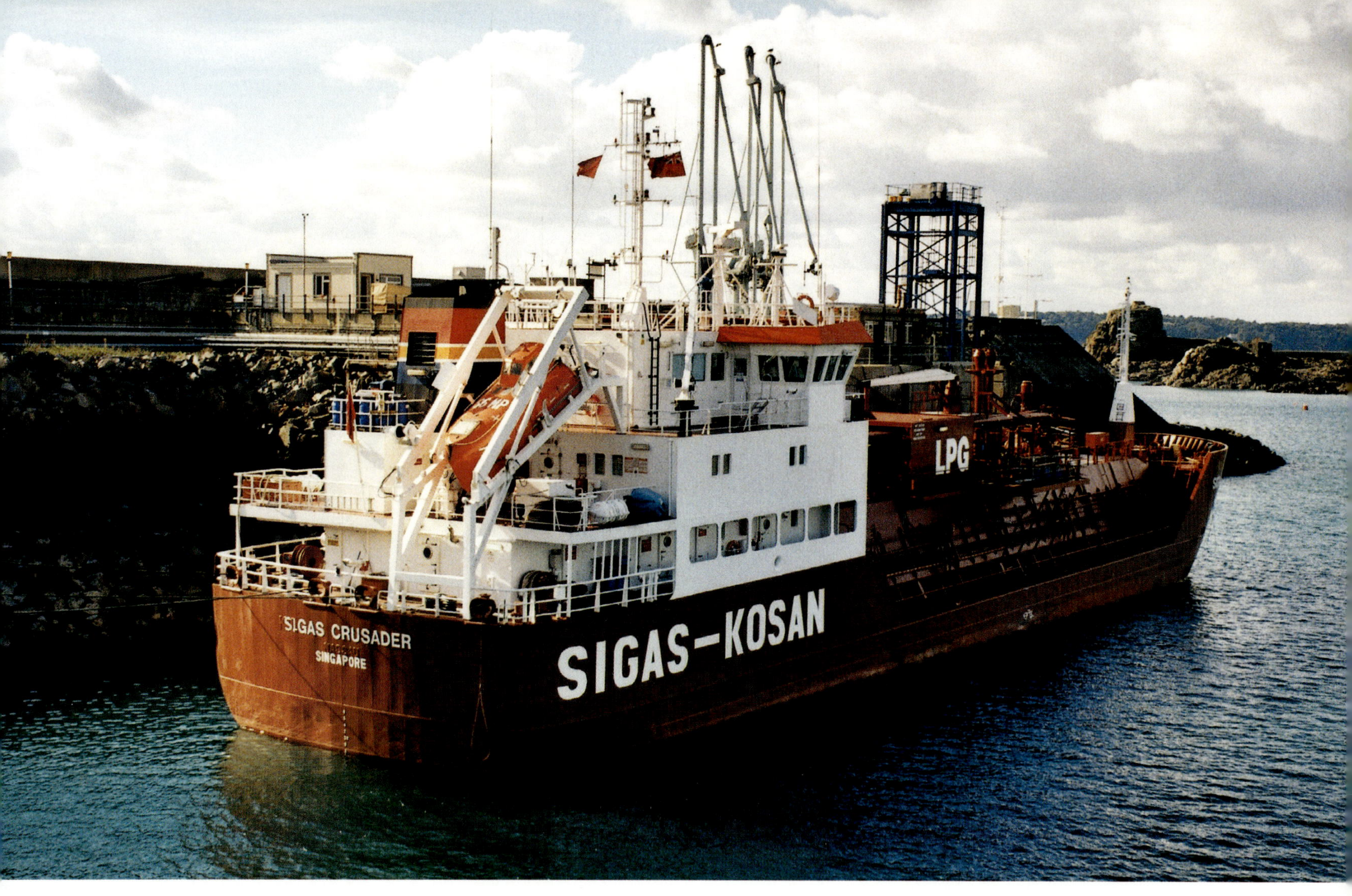

A long way from her port of registry, Singapore, the ***Sigas Crusader*** (SGP, 2458gt/96) is discharging a part cargo of liquefied petroleum gas (lpg) at St Helier's tanker berth at La Colette on 24 October 2003. She had brought her cargo from the Esso refinery at Fawley for Jersey Gas and later sailed on to St Sampson's, Guernsey, where the remainder of her cargo will be discharged for Guernsey Gas (see pages 64 - 66). One of three sisterships, she was built at the Frederikshavn yard of Ørskov Christensens Staalskibsværft as ***Kilgas Crusader***, her change of name coming in 2001. Owned by KIL Singapore Pte Ltd and managed by Tschudi & Eitzen A/S of Denmark, she has an all-Russian crew thus making her a truly international ship.

(Dave Hocquard)

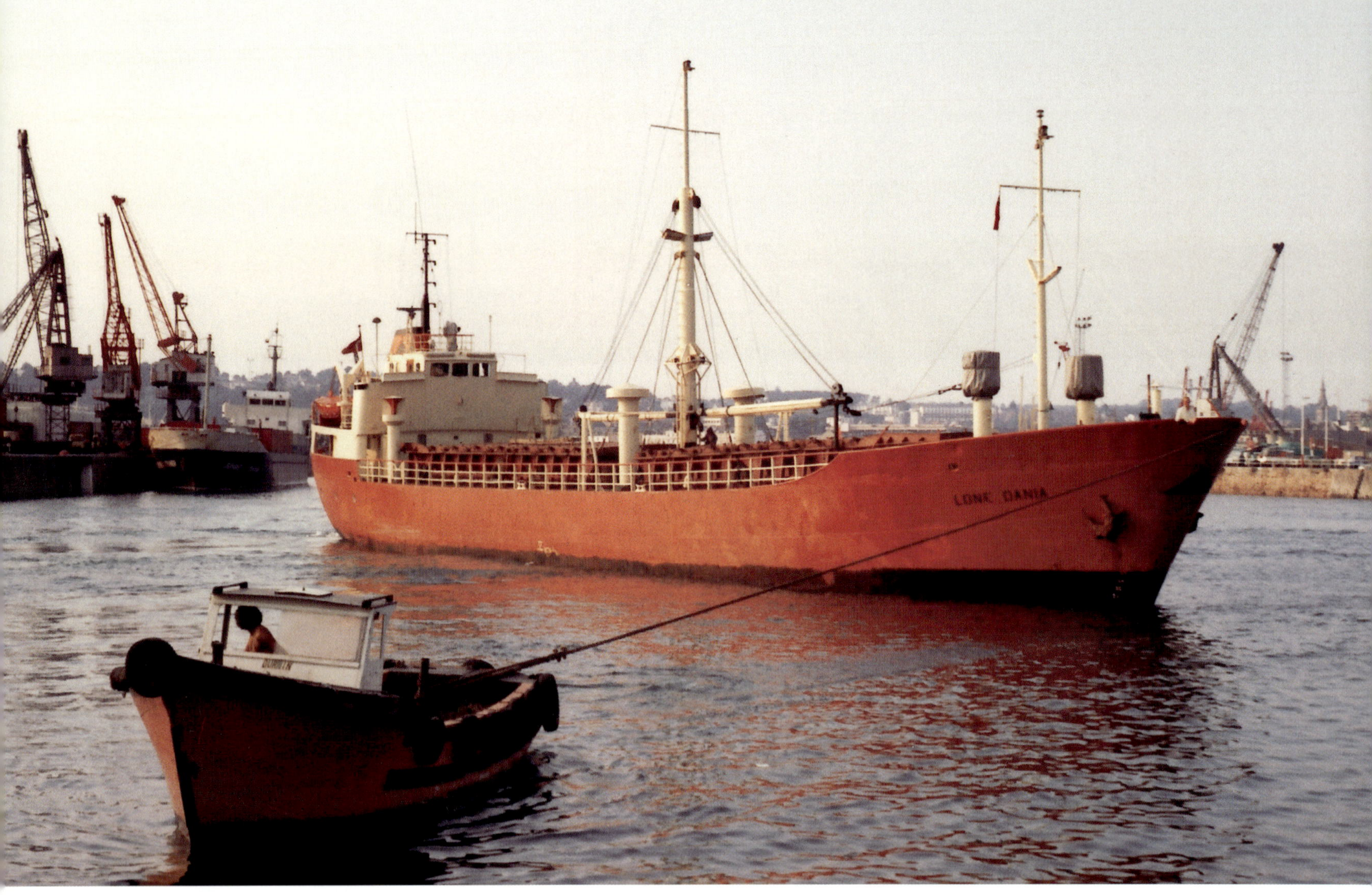

The ***Lone Dania*** (DIS, 300grt/68) is assisted into the London Boat berth in St Helier on a bright summer evening in the 1970s by the boatman's launch ***Oursin***. The ***Lone Dania*** was one of a large group of shelterdeck coasters built by Båtservice Verft A/S of Mandal (Norway), mostly for Danish and Norwegian owners in the late 1960s and early 1970s. She was sold to Cypriot flag owners in 1983 under the name ***Dimaratos***. In 1992 she was renamed ***Al-Kahir 1*** by Al Kahir Shipping & Trading Co Ltd and registered in Valletta. She was last reported to be trading as ***Al Qasim*** in 2003 having been called ***Robiyah*** for an unspecified period of time. She remains in the 2006/07 edition of *Lloyd's Register* but without any details of owner, flag or port of registry.

(Dave Hocquard)

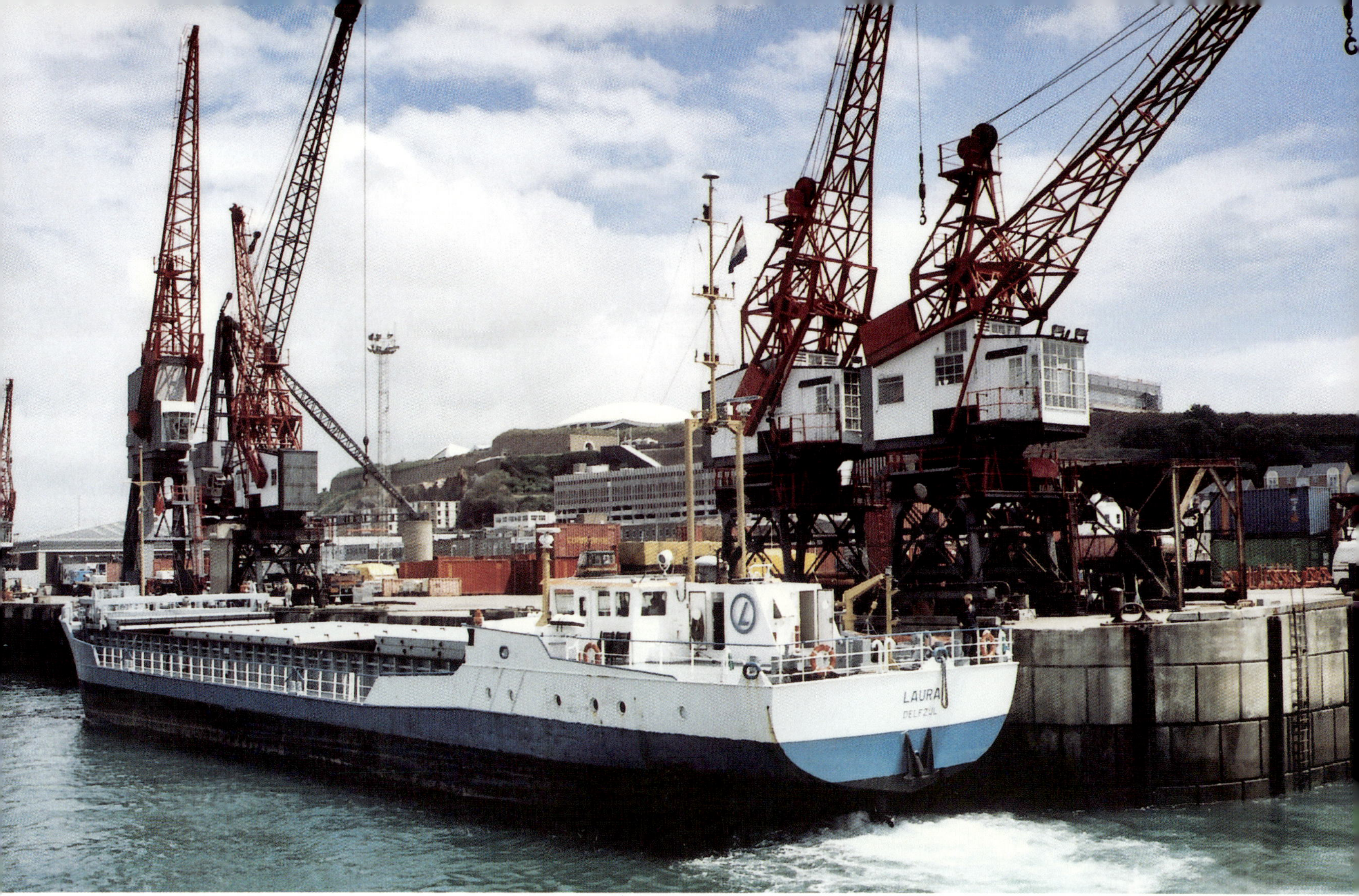

Moving from Berth 6 to Berth 7 on 2 July 1991, the Dutch flag low air draught coaster ***Laura*** (920gt/86), recently arrived in ballast from Teignmouth, is about to start loading scrap metal for northern Spain. Behind the harbour cranes is Fort Regent, now converted into a sports and leisure centre dominating St Helier and its harbour. The ***Laura*** was a product of the Ferus Smit yard at Foxhol and was managed by Wagenborg. In 1993 she changed hands within Holland and was renamed ***Sayonara*** but still managed by well-known Dutch ship operating and transport company Wagenborg. In 1999, she was renamed ***Hera*** and the ***Noordzee***, still remaining in Wagenborg management.

(Dave Hocquard)

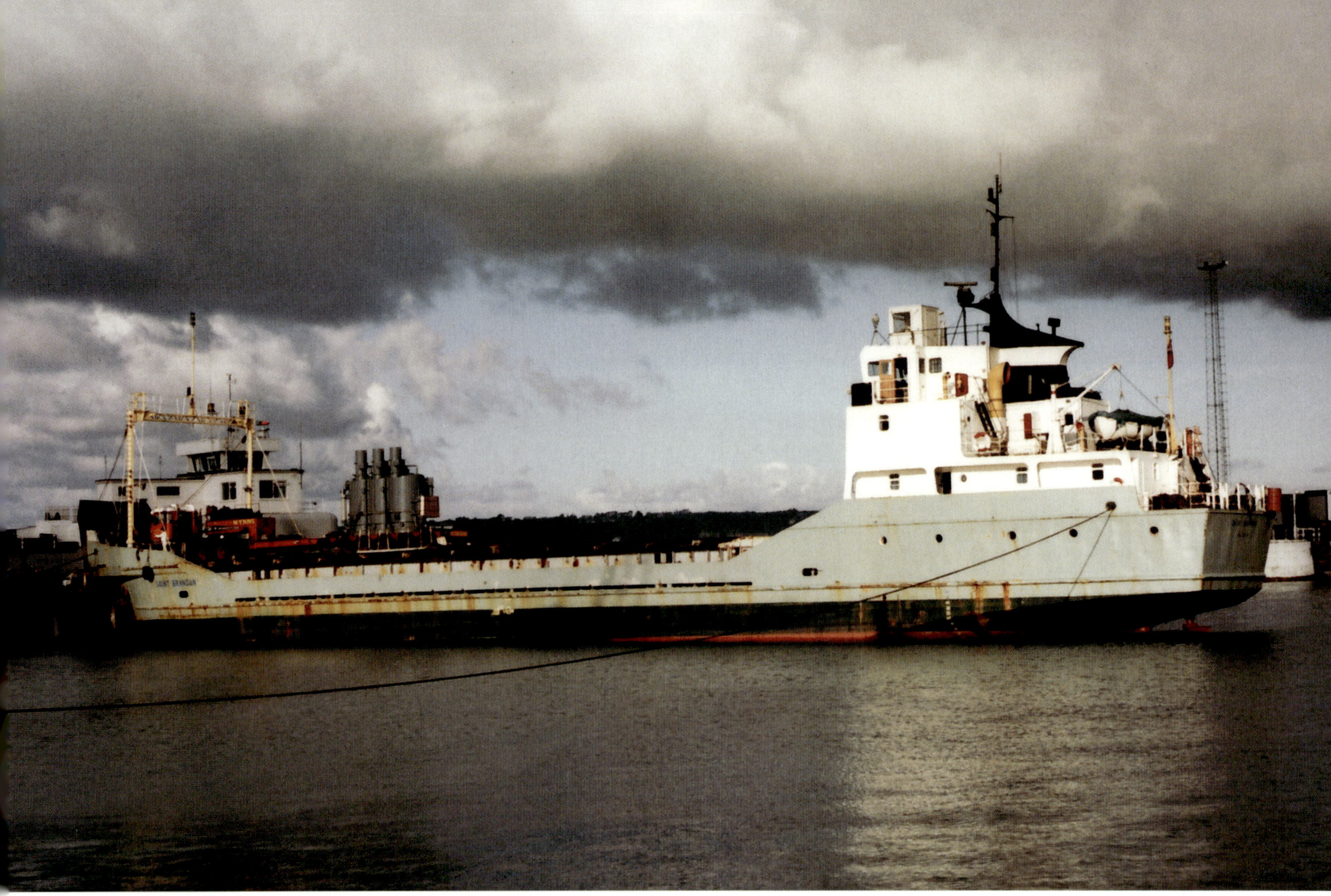

The only roll-on / roll-off vessel to appear in this book but still a genuine coaster, the ***Saint Brandan*** (GBR, 931grt/76) was owned by J & A Gardner & Co Ltd, of Glasgow. On the morning tide of 27 October 1984 and beneath a threatening sky, she is rolling two heavy transformers onto the Victoria Pier for the nearby power station. The ***Saint Brandan*** was another product of the James W Cook yard at Wivenhoe. A much travelled ship, she has had several tours of duty in the Falkland Islands on charter to the British Government.

(Dave Hocquard)

Presently the Channel Islands' longest serving ship, the bulk cement carrier ***Ronez*** (GBR, 870gt/82) is the only large ship registered in Exeter. She is seen here discharging cement at the East Cross berth on the Victoria Pier in very stormy conditions in the mid-1990s. She is believed to have been the first purpose-built bulk cement carrier for service in home waters and was constructed in Holland by Scheepswerf van Goor Monnickendam B.V. of Monnickendam.

(Dave Hocquard)

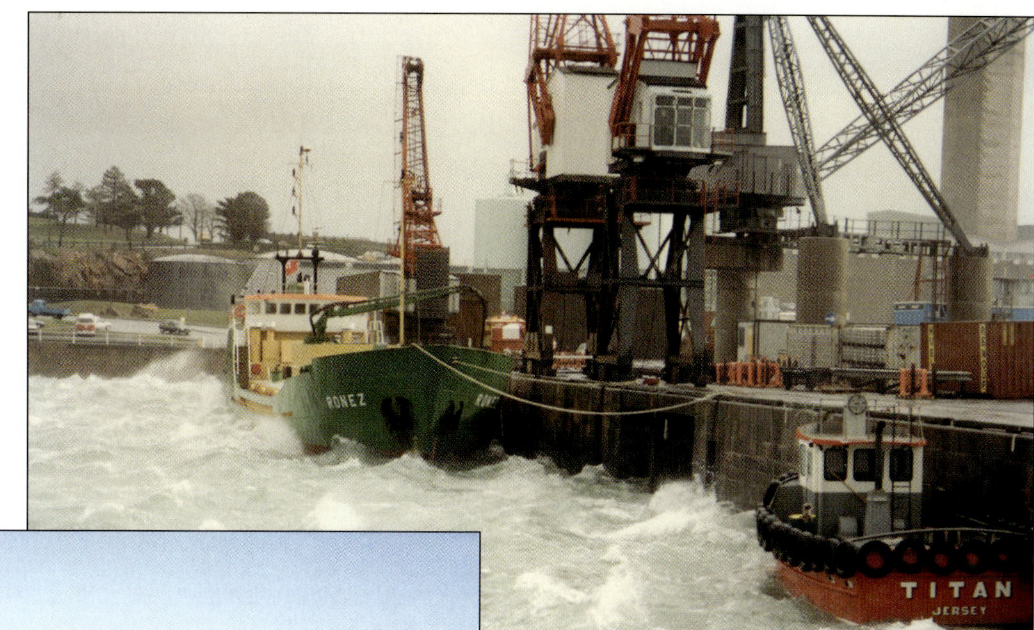

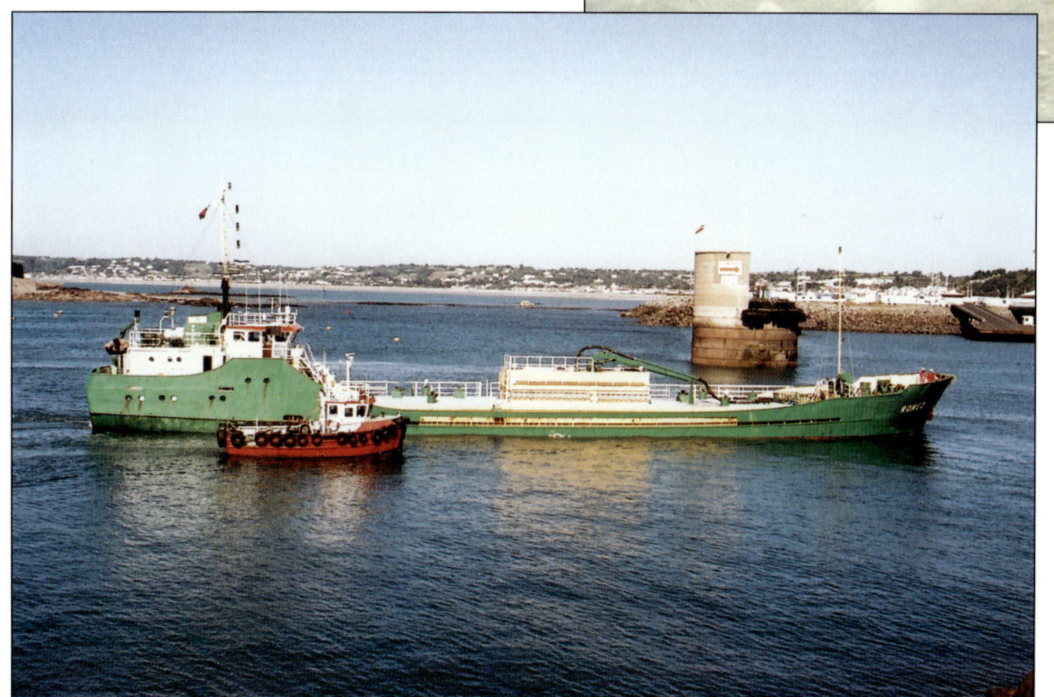

The weather conditions are very different indeed as the ***Ronez*** approaches St Helier on 23 September 2006.

(Dave Hocquard)

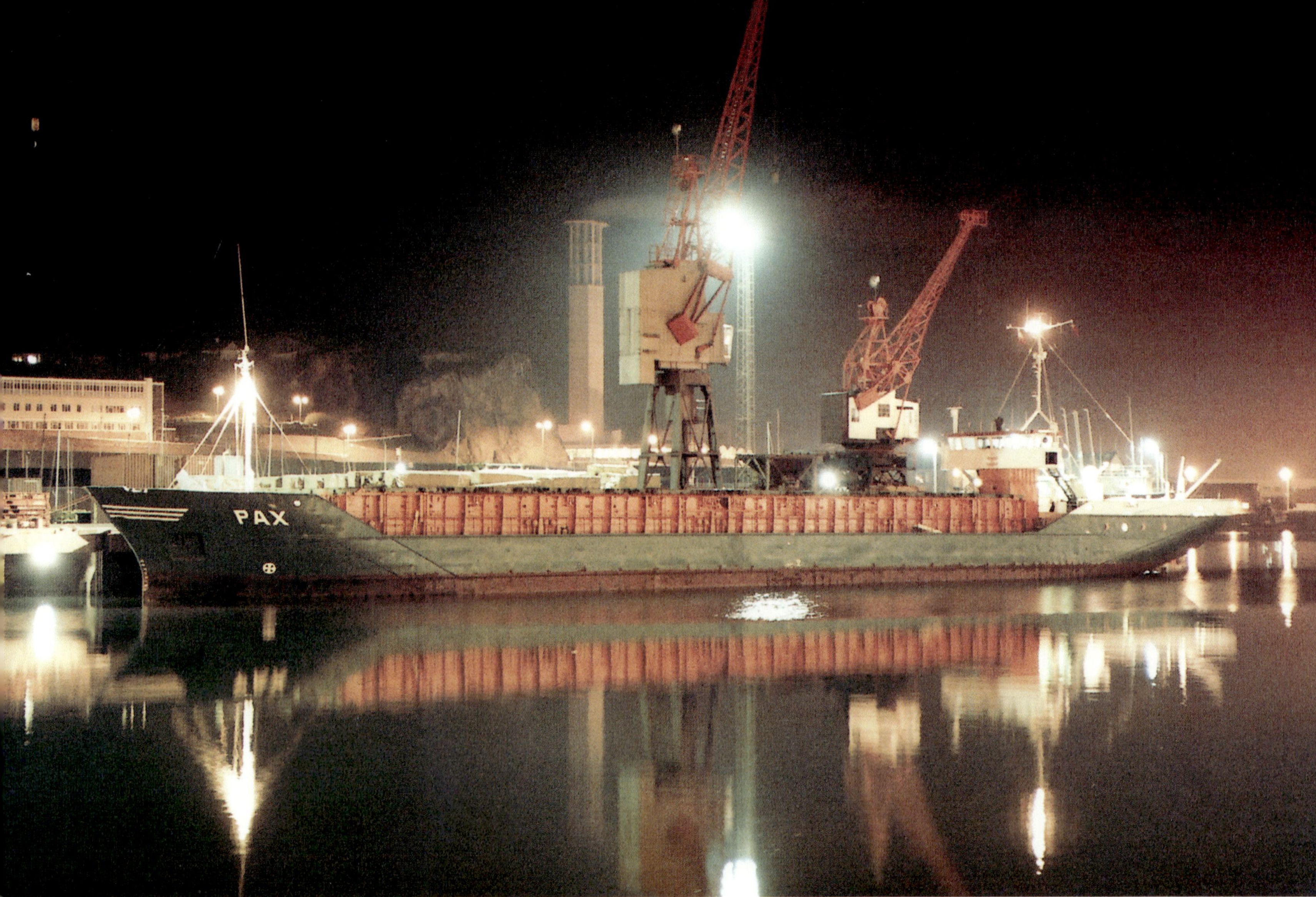

With a tidal harbour it is rare to be able to get a good night time photograph. The ***Pax*** (DIS, 1499gt/81) arrived in St Helier Harbour from Kotka via St Peter Port on 17 March 1998 with packaged timber. She is seen lying at No 6 berth on the New North Quay, one of only two berths still in commercial use on this pier. In the background is the floodlit chimney of the power station. The ***Pax*** is one of a successful series of low air draught coasters from the Peterswerft yard at Wewelsfleth during the 1980s.

(Dave Hocquard)

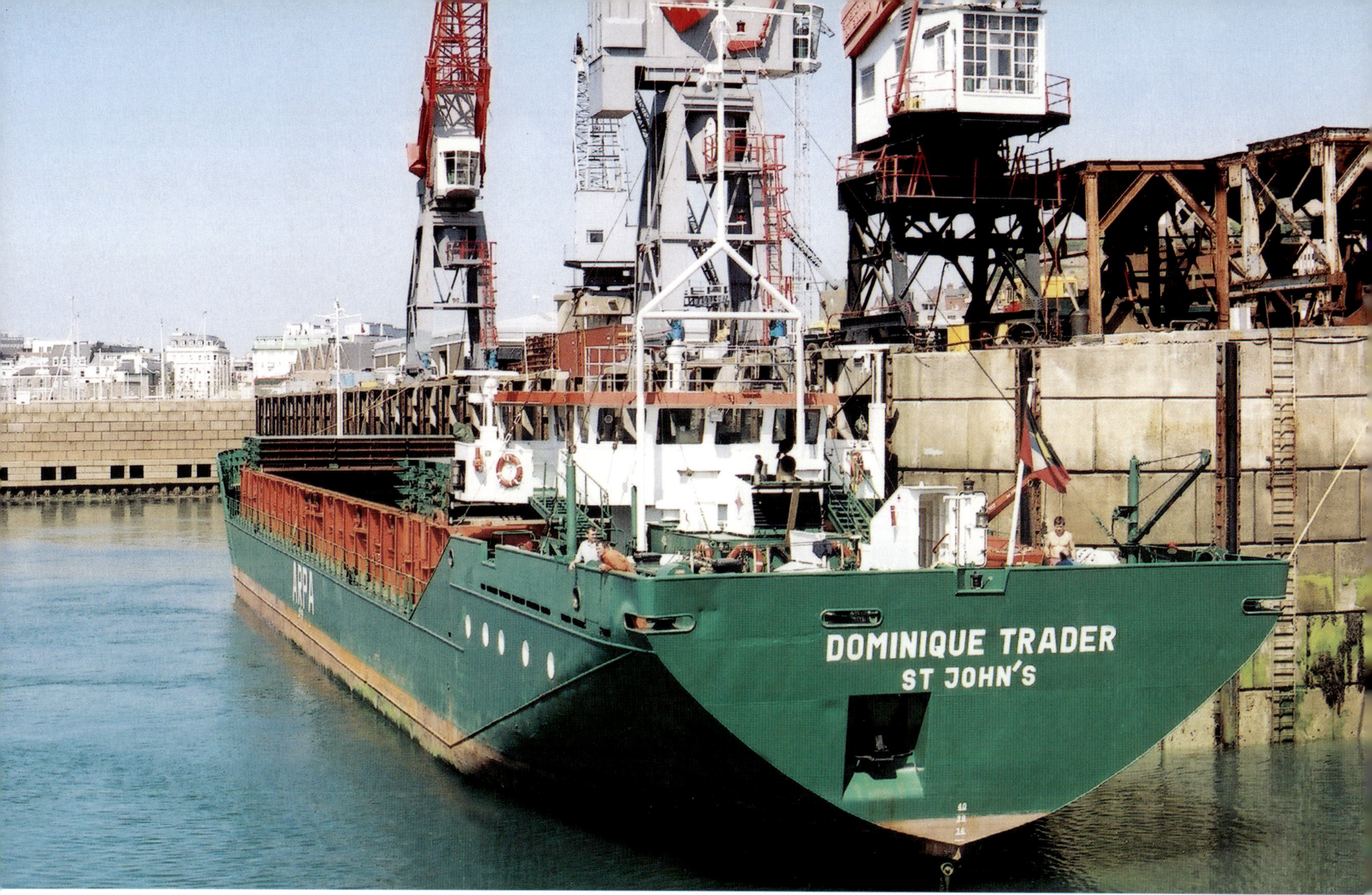

It is appropriate that we see the ***Dominique Trader*** (ATG, 1521gt/85) at the same berth but photographed under very different circumstances on 15 July 2002. She is a later example in the series of low air draught coasters from the Peterswerft yard. She was built as ***Pero*** and was renamed ***Provence*** in 1996. She became ***Dominique Trader*** after entering the Arpa Shipping fleet in 1998. In late August 2004, she left the Arpa fleet and was renamed ***Oblix*** but this name remained for only nine months for at the end of May 2005, she became ***Acer*** in the fleet of Nyki Shipping.

(Dominic McCall)

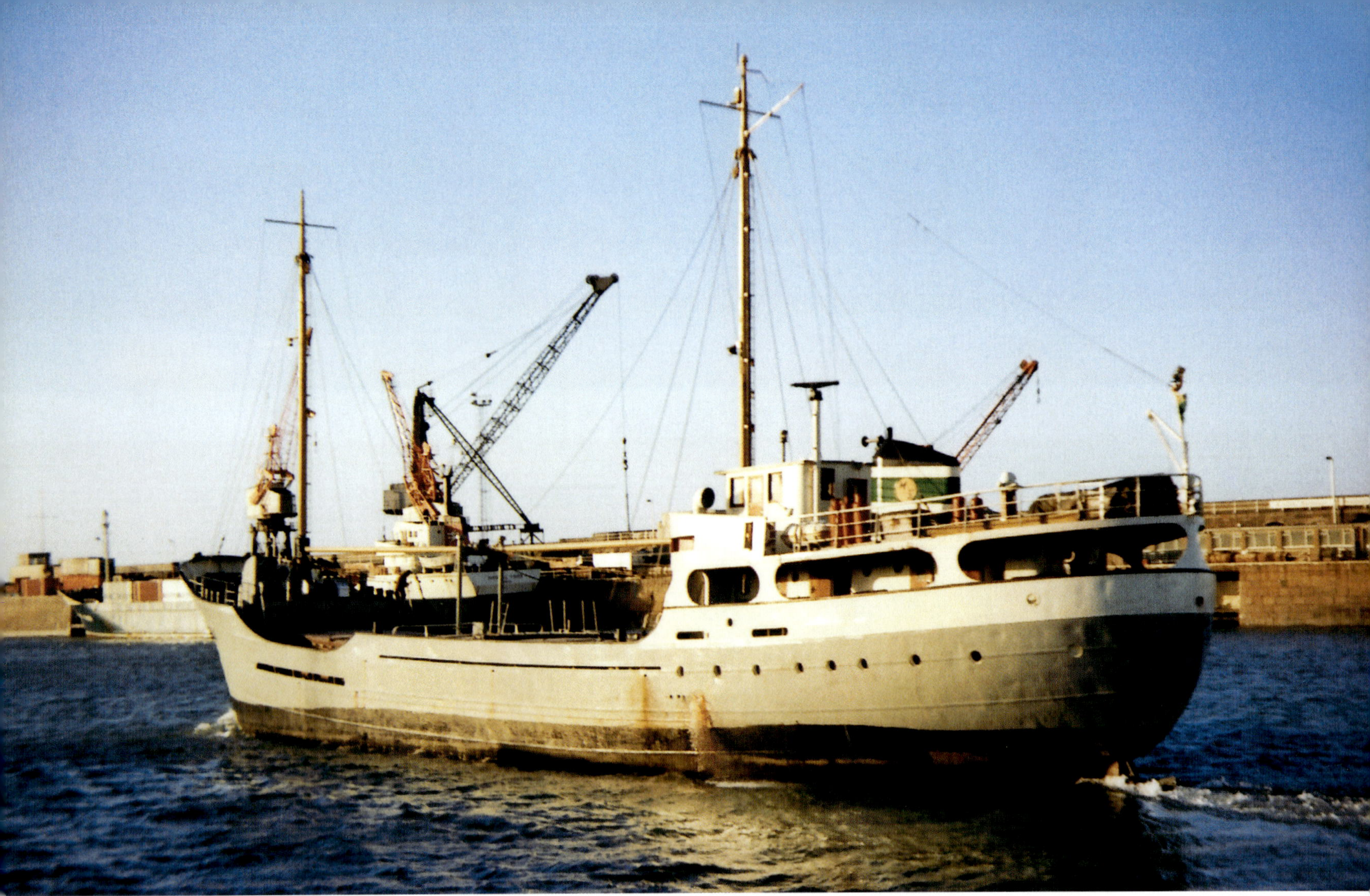

Outward bound in ballast from St Helier in the early morning winter sunshine on 4 December 1972, the Irish-flagged ***Isola*** (398grt/54) was owned at the time by Merrion Shipping Ltd, of Dublin, which had acquired her in July 1971 from Dutch owners W Meulman and Erven A Klugkist, of Groningen, without change of name. She was sold again in 1973 and renamed ***Colpro Adventurer***, becoming ***Ravenstonedale*** in 1974, ***Kingba*** in1976 and then ***Mys-Du*** in 1980. She was renamed ***Al Jumeirah*** and then ***Fawzan*** in 1992 but had disappeared from *Lloyd's Register* a decade later. In the background at No 2 berth on the Albert Pier is James Fisher's ***Jersey Fisher*** (GBR, 829grt/71) on charter to Sealink. The Scotch derrick on the quayside was later moved across the harbour to the Victoria Pier.

(Derick Goubert)

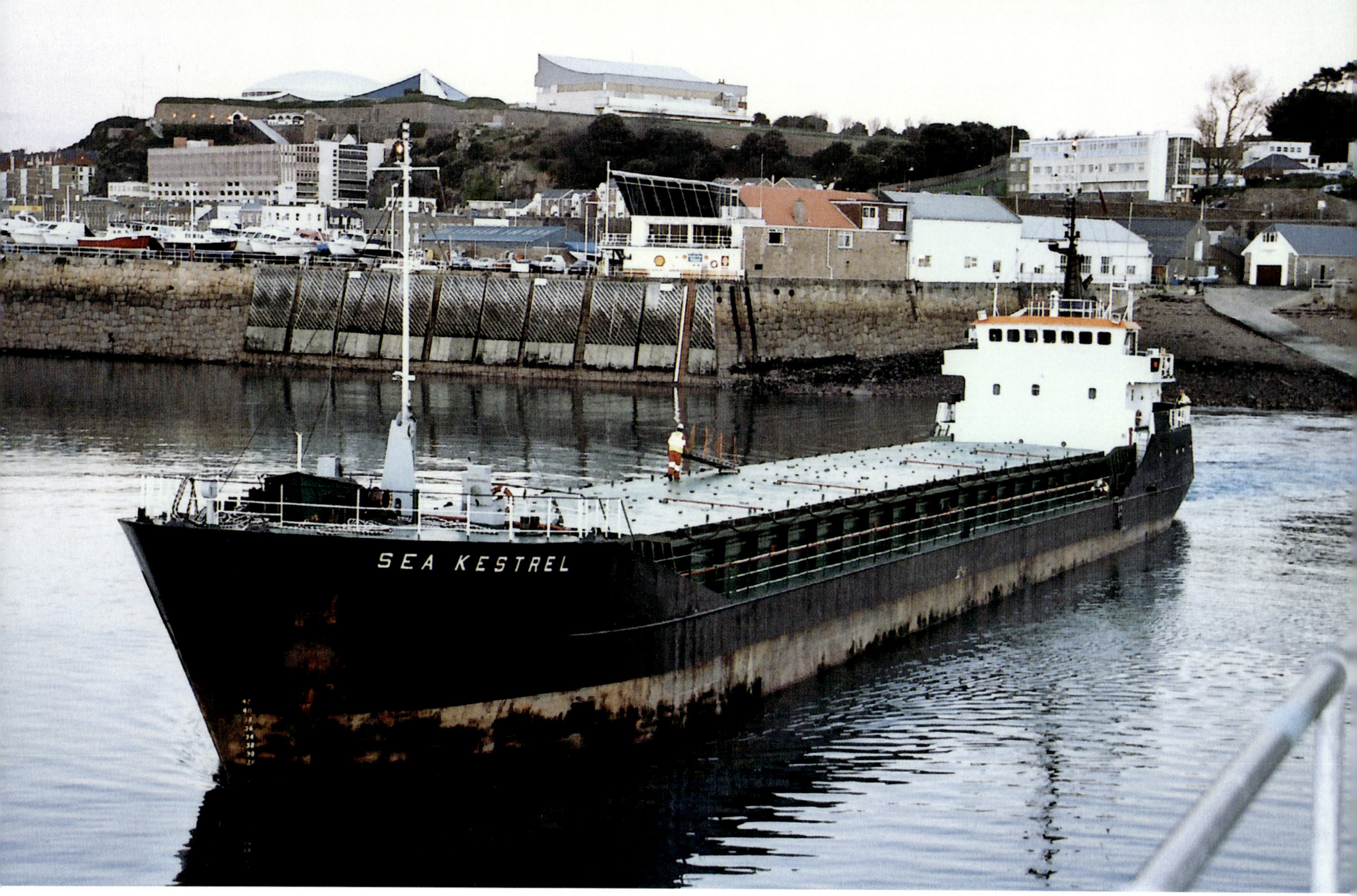

Looking more like a clear calm summer evening than 16.28 on 19 December 2005, the ***Sea Kestrel*** (BRB, 1382gt/93), having discharged a part cargo of fertiliser from Ellesmere Port, is outward bound for Guernsey where she will discharge the last few hundred tons. In the background is South Pier with pleasure boats laid up for the winter, the yacht refuelling berths, futuristic frontage of St Helier Yacht Clubhouse and Fort Regent Leisure Centre on the hill. Owned by BUE Marine Ltd, the ***Sea Kestrel*** was previously Lapthorn's ***Hoo Kestrel***. She is one of three sisterships built for Lapthorn by the Yorkshire Dry Dock company in Hull.

(Dave Hocquard)

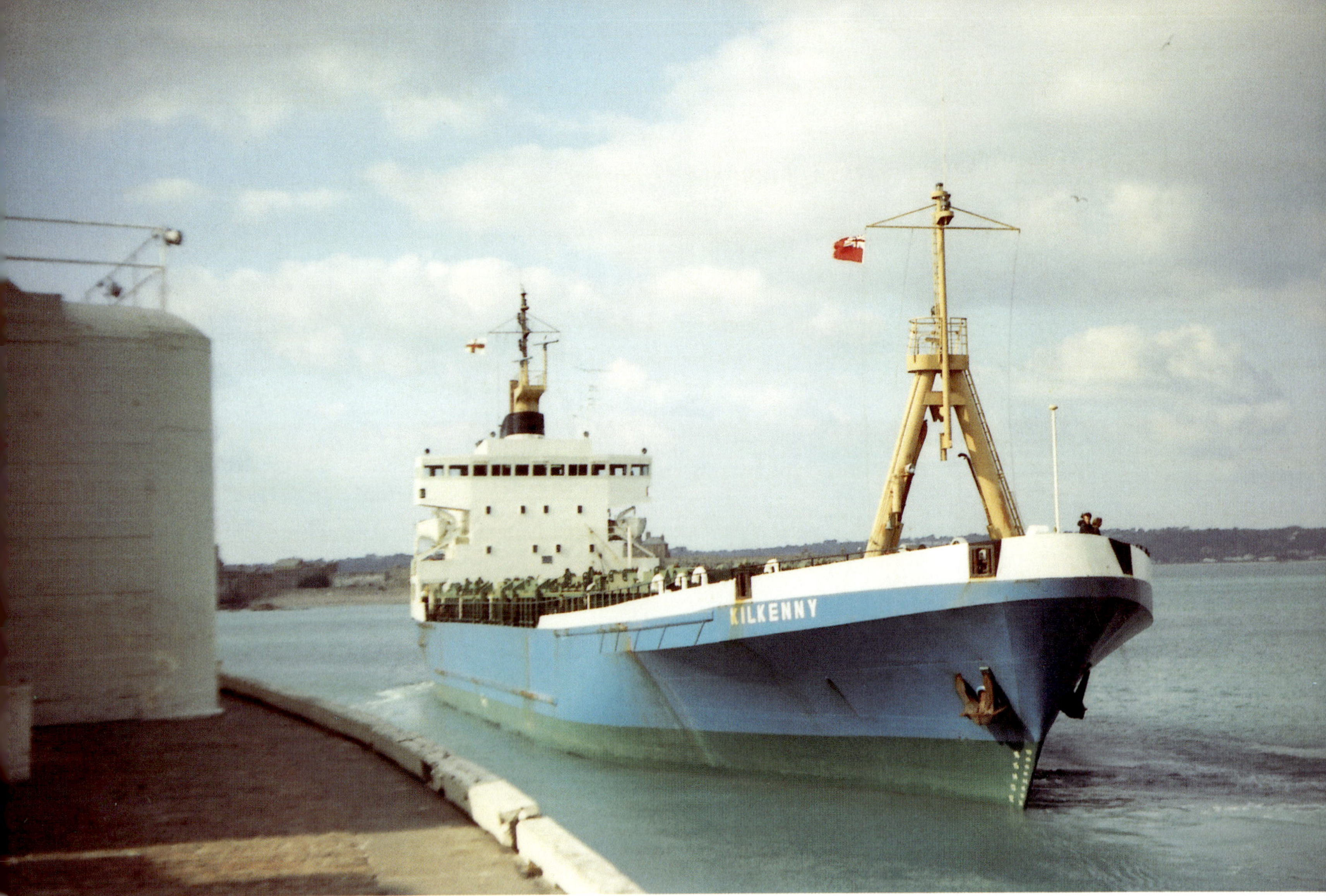

Seen backing out of St Helier Harbour having discharged her cargo of Irish peat moss in containers, B. & I.'s ***Kilkenny*** (1514grt/73), built at Cork by the Verolme Cork Dockyard Ltd. At 99,60 m long, she was one of the largest cargo vessels to use St Helier Harbour. This manoeuvre would be very difficult today now that the Elizabeth Ferry Terminal has been built. Sadly the ***Kilkenny*** sank in Dublin Bay on 21 November 1991 after being in collision with the ***Hasselwerder*** (DEU, 3329grt/84). Her wreck was later removed by the German salvage firm of Bugsier and broken up in Holland.

(Dave Hocquard)

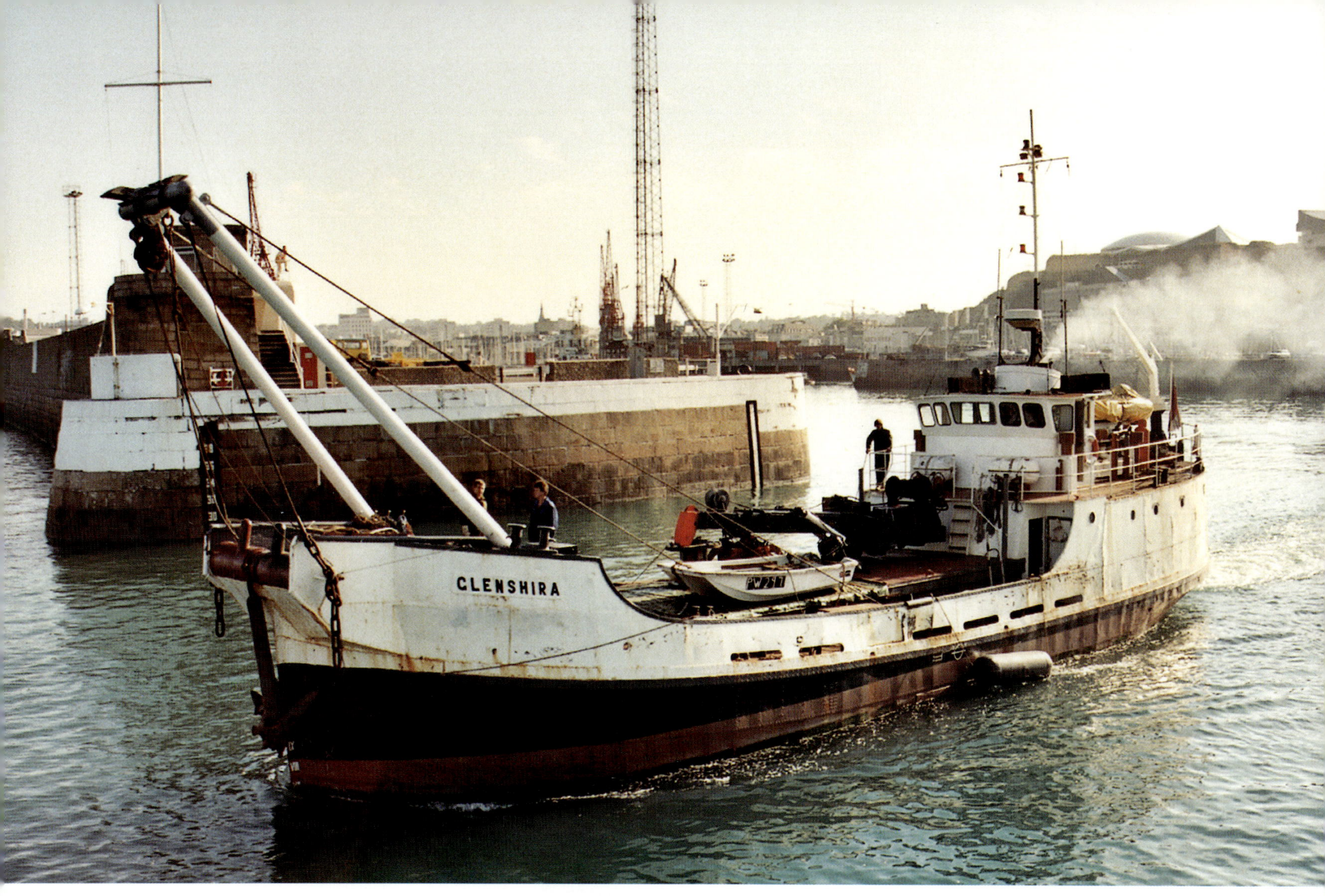

No longer really a coaster, the ***Glenshira*** (GBR, 149grt/53) was a former motor "puffer" which was later fitted out as a salvage vessel. She is seen outward bound on the morning of 11 July 1990 after taking on stores and bunkers. On this voyage she was returning to the area south-east of Sark to continue salvage work to recover cargo from the wreck of the French steamer ***Jeanne Marie*** (2971grt), mined and sunk on 14 March 1918 while bound from New York and Brest for Le Havre with a cargo of copper ingots. At the time, the ***Glenshira*** was owned by Capt. Frank Saunders and others of Southampton. She was built at Bowling on the River Clyde by Scott & Sons for G & G Hamilton Ltd, of Glasgow. She had many owners over the years including Peter Herbert, of Bude.

(Robert Le Maistre)

Photographed from a lower vantage point on a sunny 8 October 1993, the ***Marico*** (CYP, 999gt/76) is outward bound having loaded scrap for northern Spain. The photo was taken from the end of the rock armour breakwater which protects the La Colette tidal marina and fish quay. It was built in the 1970s and now is an ideal place to photograph ships at almost any time but best before early afternoon when this photo was taken. Built by Scheepswerf "Voorwaarts" at Hoogezand, the ***Marico*** was under Wagenborg management at the time of the photograph, her former names being ***Gina P*** until 1992, ***Kwintebank*** until 1984 and ***Els Teekman*** until 1984. In 1995 she became ***Jamie*** and then ***Aunborg*** three years later.

(Dave Hocquard)

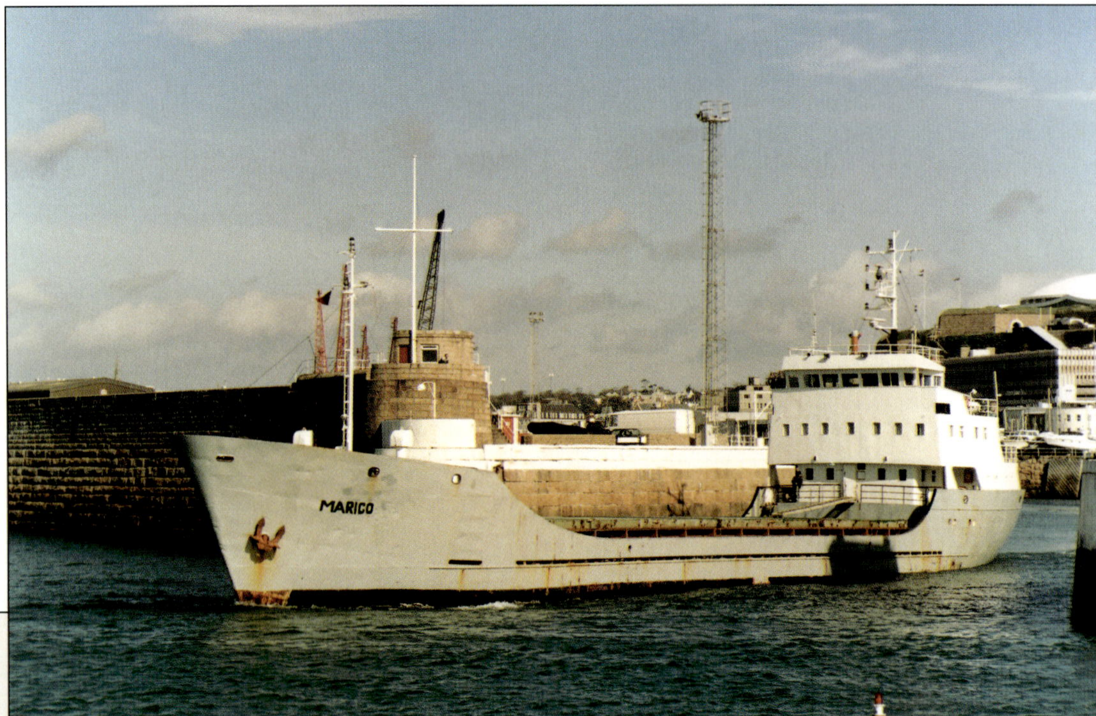

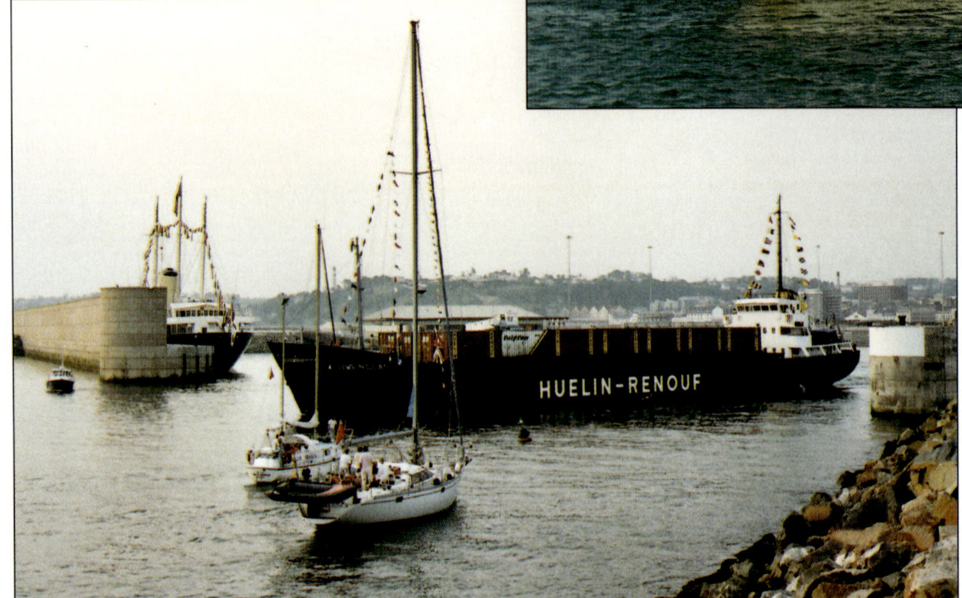

On 24 May 1989, the ***Owenglas*** (PAN, 763grt/70) is outward bound for Portsmouth while on charter to Huelin Shipping Services, of Jersey, and is dressed overall for a royal occasion. Her Majesty The Queen and Prince Philip were in Jersey to open the new Queen Elizabeth ro/ro berths and passenger terminal seen in the background with the Royal Yacht ***Britannia*** in the west berth. The ***Owenglas*** began her long association with the Channel Islands in April 1975 when on charter to Commodore and ended in July 1991 with her charter to Huelin Renouf. This view shows clearly the location for the two previous photographs. The ***Owenglas*** was built by Scheepswerf Hoogezand. In 1991, she was sold to Arab owners, converted to a livestock carrier and renamed ***Safad***. After four further changes of name, she appears to be still trading in the Middle East though now flying the flag of North Korea and named ***Ahmad N***.

(Dave Hocquard)

The Master's view of a departure from St Helier's Berth 7 as the ***Isis*** pulls away from the quayside and Huelin Renouf's ***Huelin Dispatch*** (BHS, 1892gt/78) lies at the inner part of the berth on 10 July 2002. The latter vessel now maintains the only regular lift on / lift off service from the UK to the Channel Islands, linking Jersey and Guernsey to Portsmouth.

(Dominic McCall)

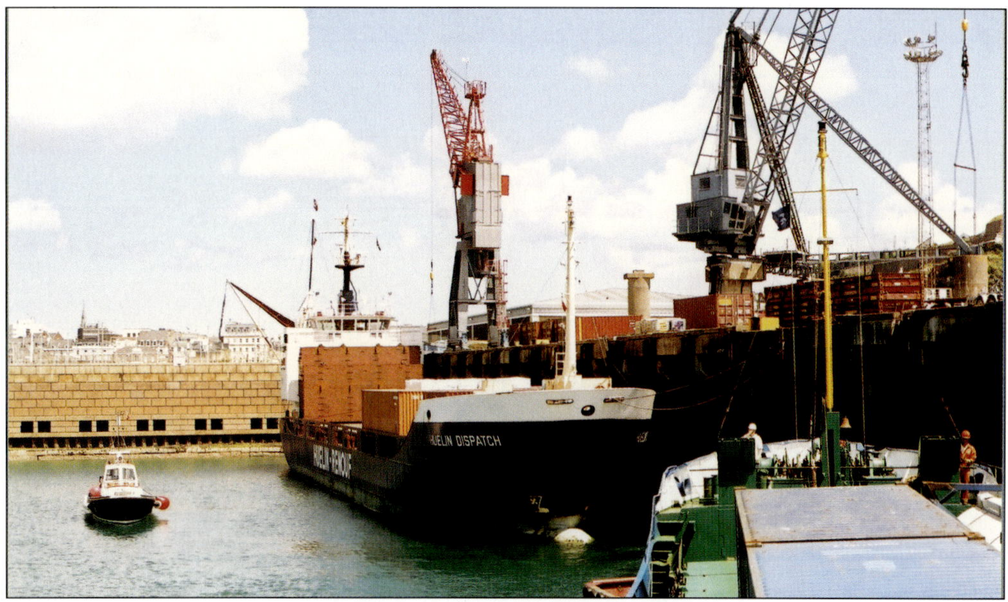

The ***Huelin Dispatch*** herself departs from Jersey on 26 June 2002 a few days prior to the photograph above. An example of the J J Sietas Type 95a design, *Lloyd's Register* notes that her aft section was built at the Norderwerft yard in Hamburg and forward section at the Sietas yard. Launched as ***Süderelv***, she traded under this name until 1991 when she was renamed ***Stenholm*** and then ***Visbur*** in the same year. In 1992, she became ***Stenholm*** once again until acquired in 1996 by Huelin-Renouf Shipping Services by whom she was renamed ***Huelin Dispatch***.

(Dominic McCall)

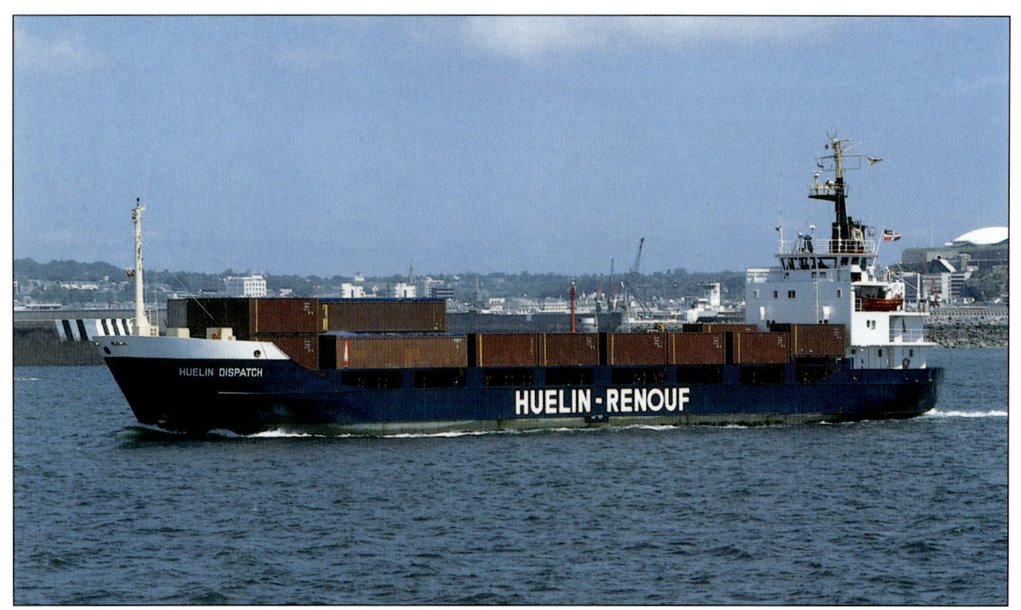

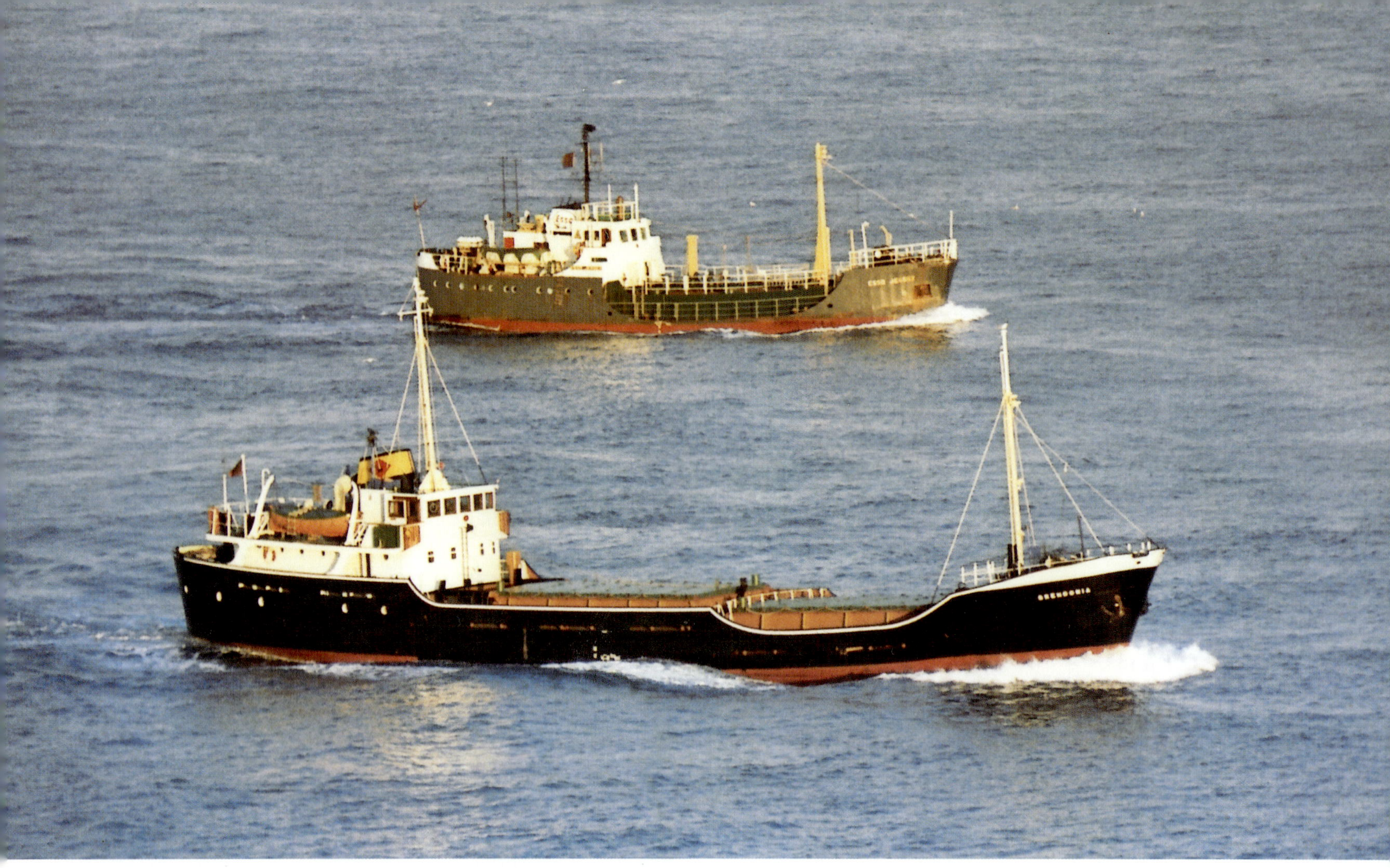

Noirmont Point, the headland on the western side of St Aubins, is an excellent point to watch ships arriving or departing from Jersey. All vessels heading west and north pass within a few hundred yards of the Point. It is especially ideal for photography on a summer evening such as 12 June 1971 when this photo was taken. The tanker ***Esso Jersey*** (GBR, 313grt/61) is outward bound in ballast for Fawley. Nearer the camera and approaching the Point is the ***Brendonia*** (GBR, 604grt/66) outward bound for Portsmouth with potatoes. The photo was taken using a 300mm zoom lens but a 200mm lens would be adequate for today's larger coasters. The ***Esso Jersey***, built at Bowling by Scott & Sons, became ***John S Darbyshire*** in 1974 and then ***Kielder*** in 1976. As such, she worked as an effluent tanker until demolished at Hull in 1984. The ***Brendonia*** was a product of Goole Shipbuilding & Repair Co Ltd. Sold and renamed ***Brendonian*** in 1984, she later became ***Shaskia Lee*** in 2000, ***Sea Song*** in 2003 and ***Ocean Song*** in 2005. She is thought to be still at work in the Caribbean.

(Dave Hocquard)

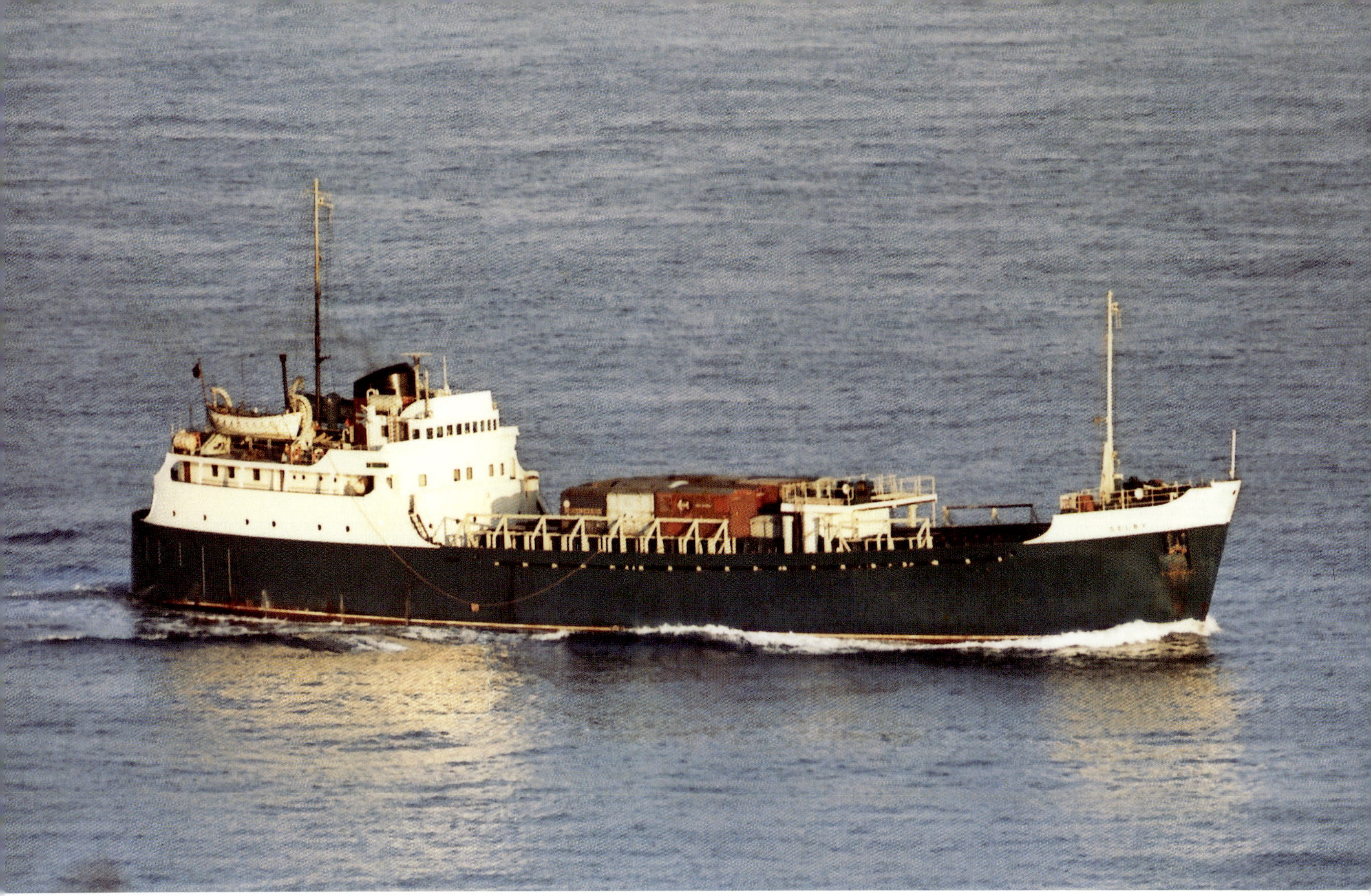

Here we see British Rail's ***Selby*** (GBR, 963grt/59) nearing Noirmont Point bathed in the last of the evening sunshine of 12 June 1971. She is bound for Southampton with produce and several of the old type of railway containers on deck. The ***Selby*** was built by James Lamont & Co Ltd, Glasgow, originally for general cargo trade but she had her large bipod mast and derricks removed in mid-1965. This modification made her more suitable to carry containers. In October 1972 she was sold to Pounds Marine Shipping Ltd who resold her to Panamanian owners the following year; she was then renamed ***Raven***. After being renamed ***Jean R*** in 1973 and ***Victory*** in 1977, she was sold to Italian shipbreakers at La Spezia in February 1981. Not demolished she was sold to trading owners in Greece and renamed ***Agios Nikolaos***. She is still listed in *Lloyd's Register* although she has not been seen in recent years.

(Dave Hocquard)

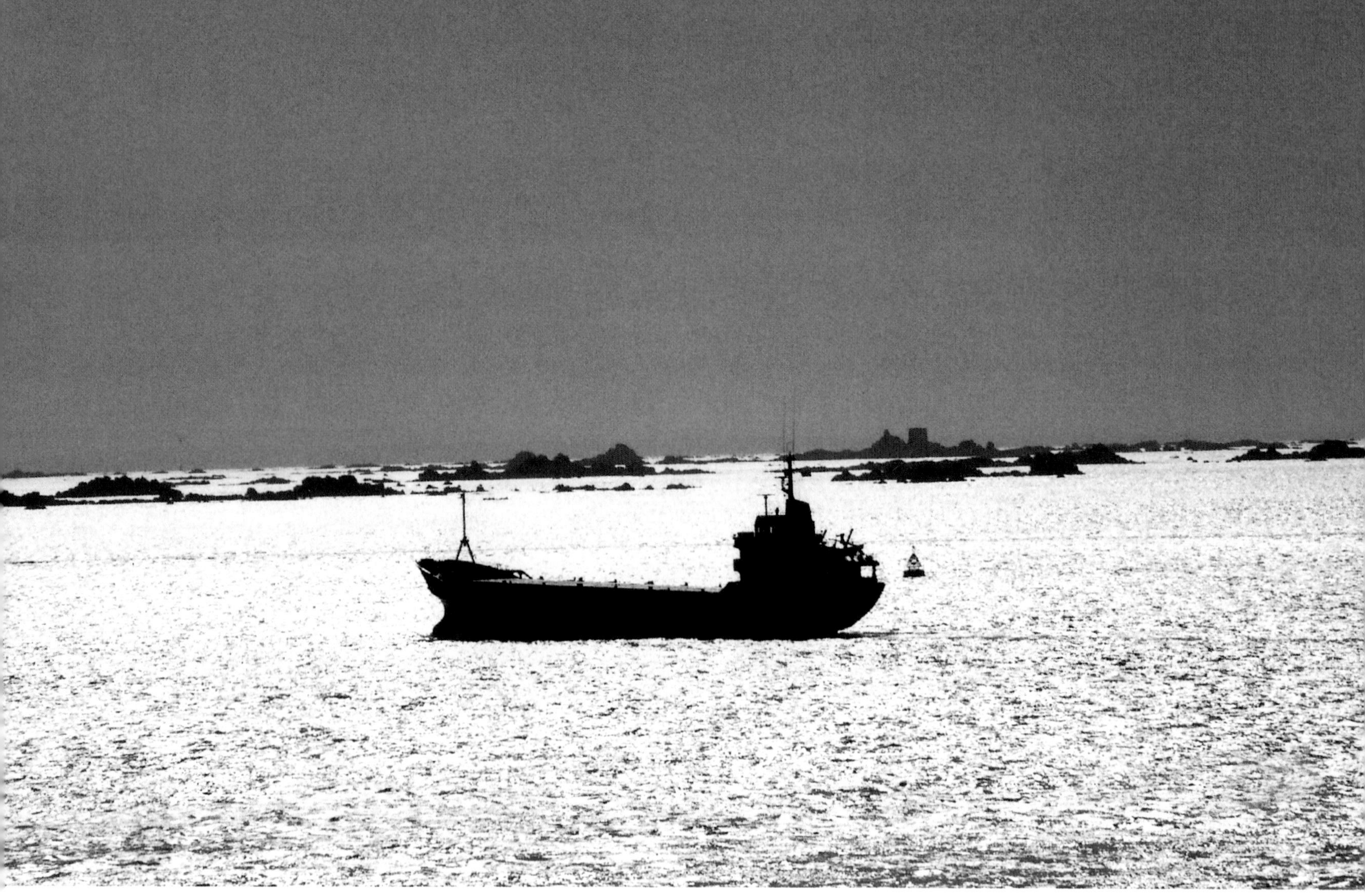

Silhouetted in the early morning sun, the ***Alcotan*** (PAN, 1254gt/76) crosses St Aubins Bay on a silver sea on 18 August 1991 inbound to St Helier in ballast from New Holland to load scrap metal for northern Spain. In the background is the massive reef of rocks to the south-east of the harbour and known as the Violet Bank. The Icho Tower, built in the early nineteenth century for the defence of the island, is in the far background standing on one of the largest rocks. The ***Alcotan***, ex ***Catalina Del Mar***-99, was built by Ast. y Talleres Celaya at Bilbao and, at the date of the photograph, owned by Brunel Shipping S. A. of Panama. She was subsequently sold to Chinese operators and renamed ***Hong Tai***, becoming ***Hai Shou Shan*** in 1995, although remaining under the flag of Panama.

(Dave Hocquard)

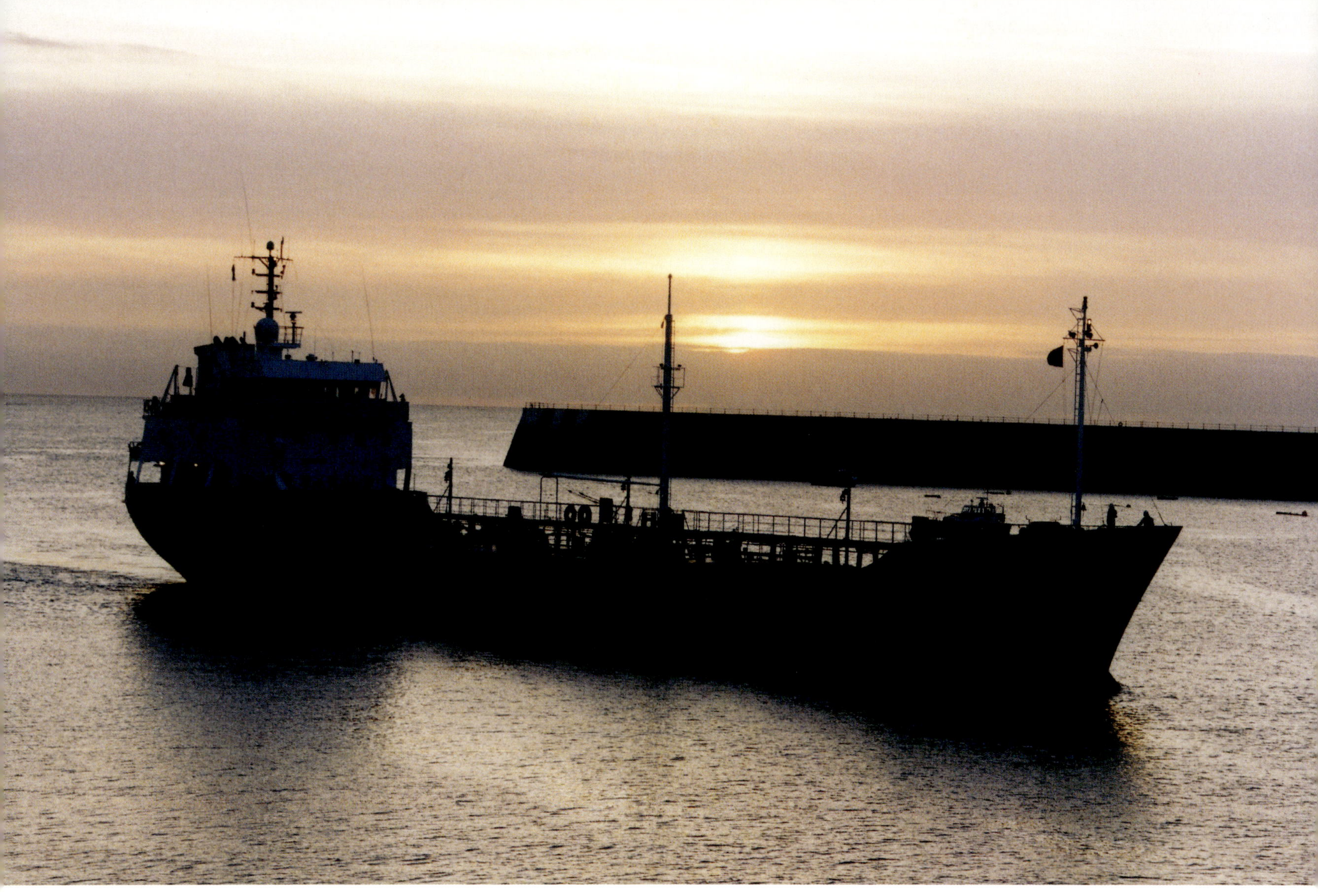

Arriving at St Helier and silhouetted in the late afternoon sunshine of 15 December 2003, the ***Stella Pollux*** (NLD, 2523gt/81) is about to turn in St Helier's "Small Roads" inside the Elizabeth Castle breakwater and go astern into the tanker basin to discharge her cargo of fuel oil. The present tank farm and tanker berth were built on land reclaimed from the foreshore in the 1970s. The tanker was built at the Nieuw Noord Nederlandse shipyard in Groningen.

(Dave Hocquard)

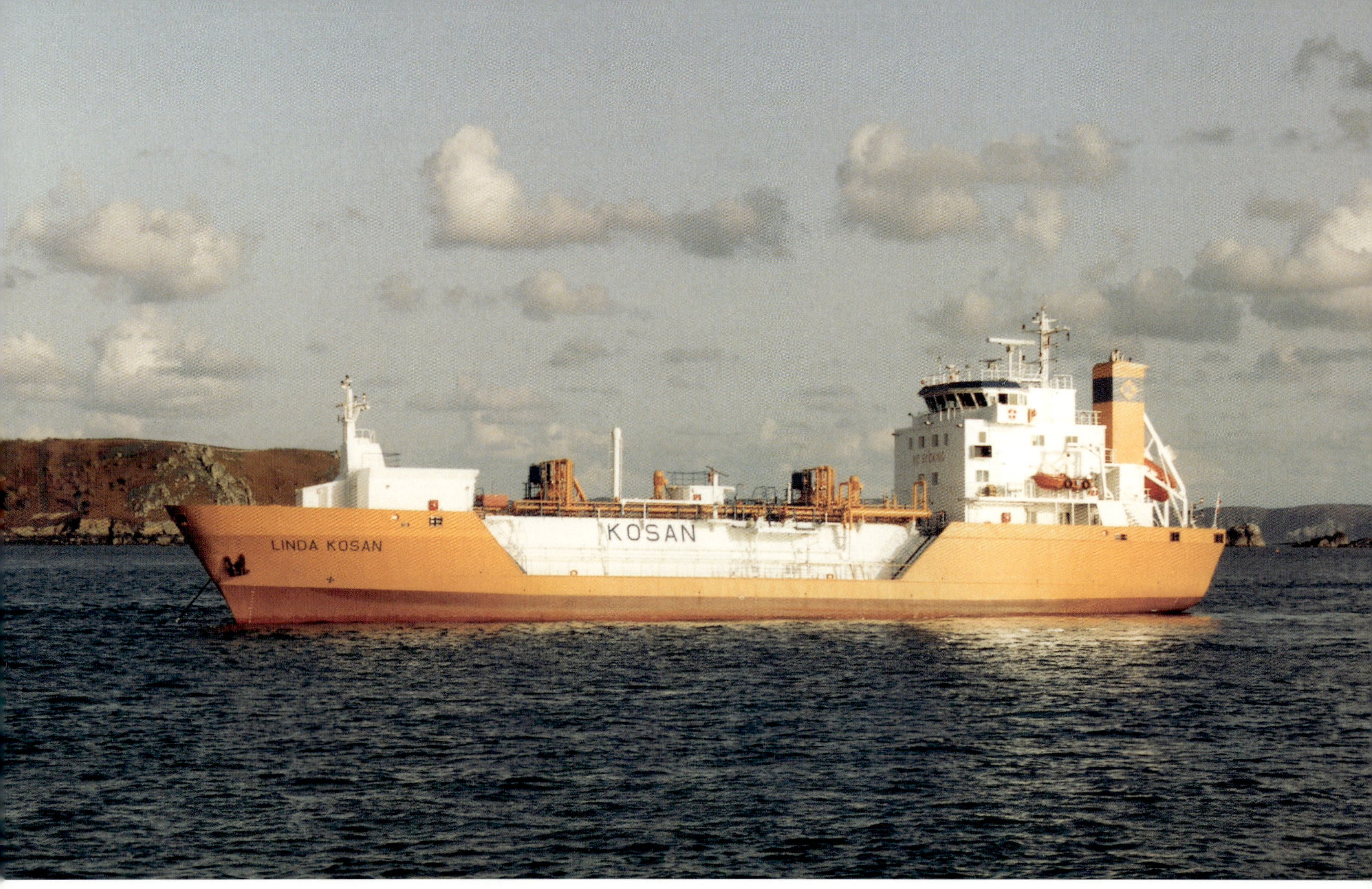

We now leave Jersey and move to Guernsey. The ***Linda Kosan*** (DIS, 2224gt/92) lies at anchor off St Peter Port bathed in evening sunlight with the small island of Jethou in the background and in the distance astern of her is Sark. Having arrived from Fawley via Jersey, she has a part cargo of lpg for Guernsey's gas undertaking and she waits the high tide to enter St Sampsons harbour. At the time still registered under the Danish flag, she changed her port of registry and flag to Douglas, Isle of Man, during early in 1994. She was built at the Hermann Sürken shipyard in Papenburg.

(the late Peter Leadbeater)

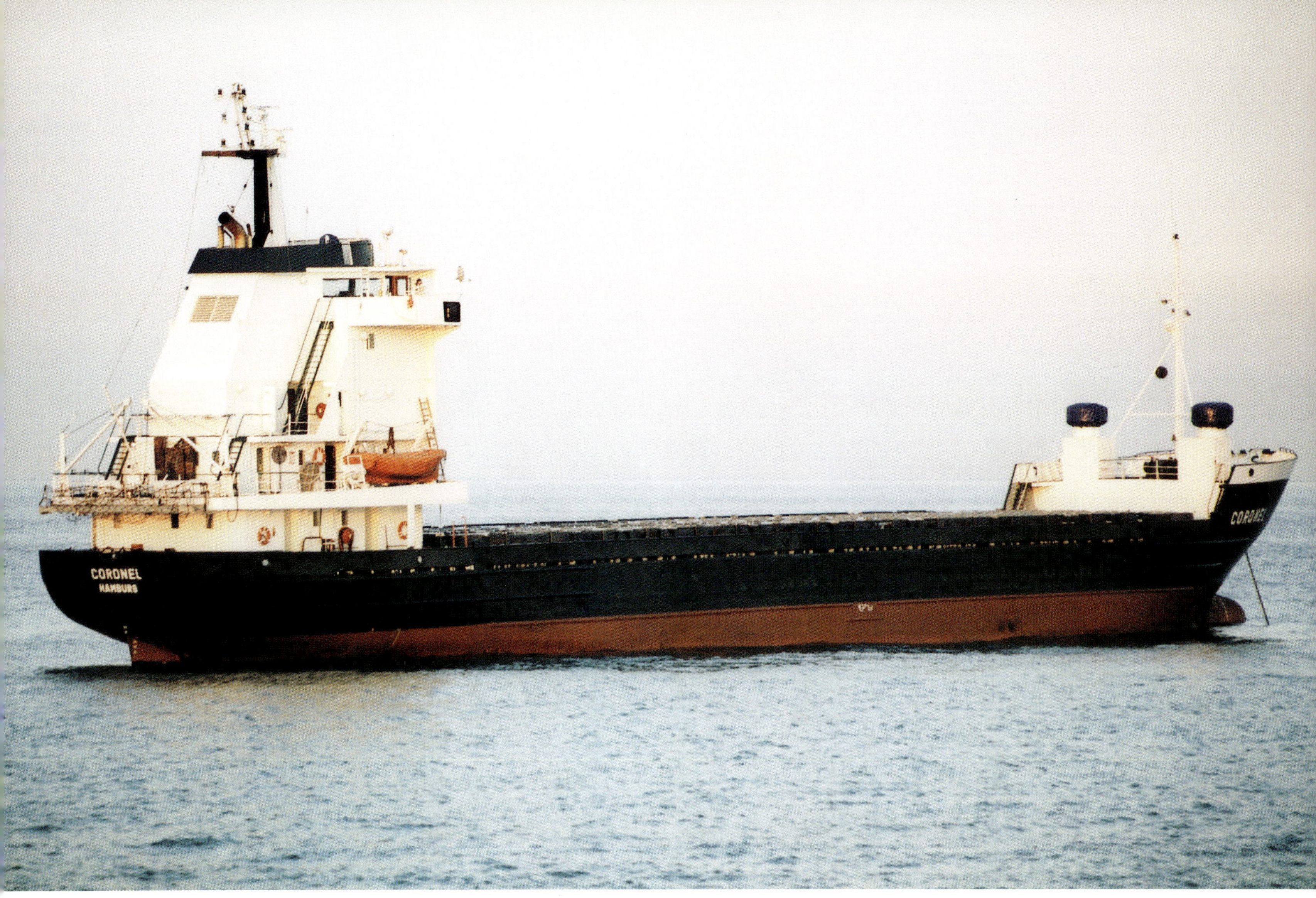

Again at anchor but off St Peter Port, the island's capital, is the ***Coronel*** (ATG, 2089gt/78). The photograph was taken in July 2000. She was built at the Hugo Peters shipyard in Wewelsfleth as ***Christel*** and took her present name in 1995. Between 1997 and 2000 she was renamed ***Lys Coronel*** for the duration of a charter to Lys Line.

(Ron Wood)

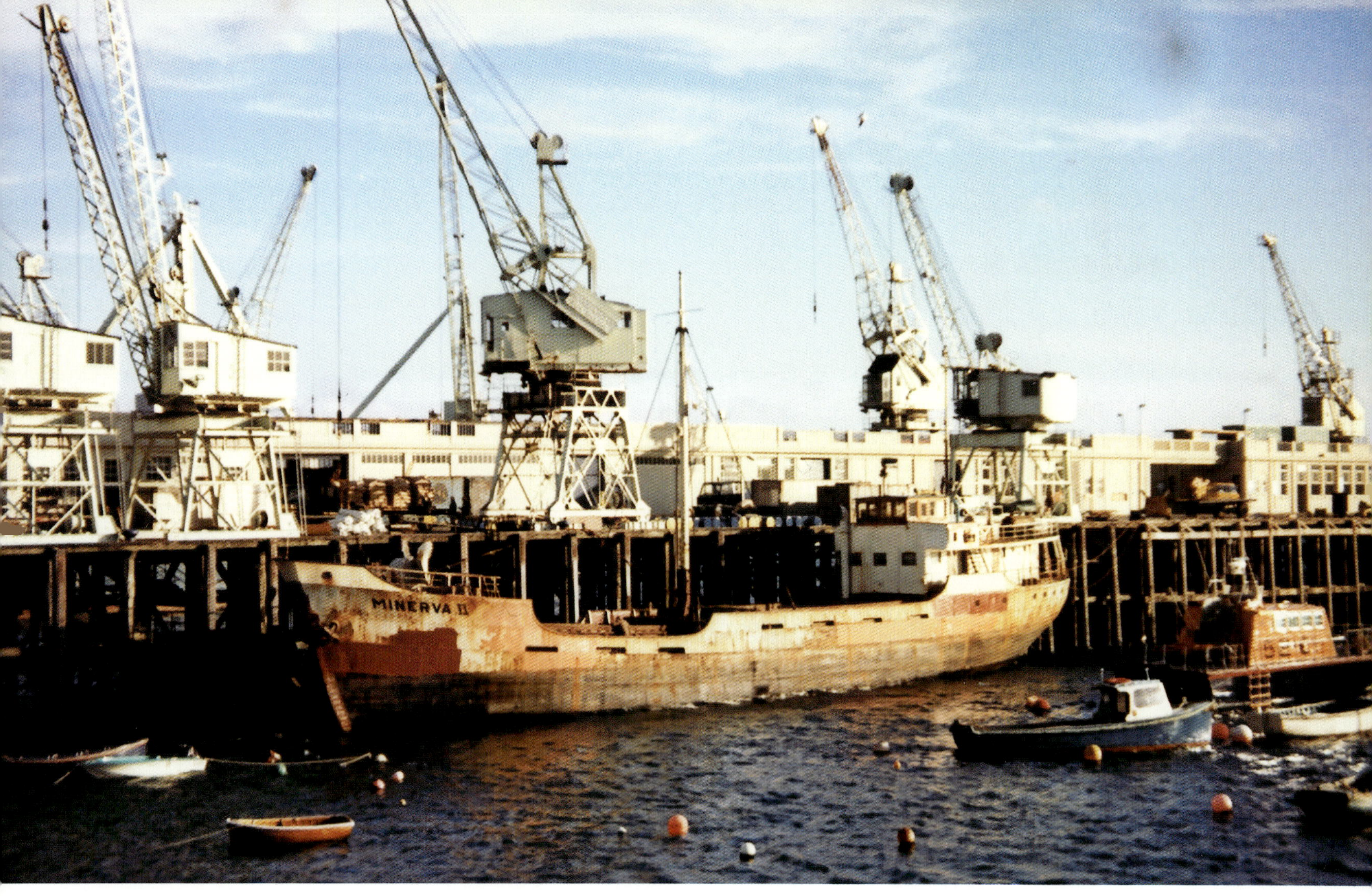

It was very unusual for a Dutch coaster to be so rusty but certainly the ***Minerva II*** (NLD, 400grt/49) was in urgent need of paint when seen here on an inside berth on St Peter Port's "New Jetty" in about 1970. What dates this view is the series of cranes built by Stothert & Pitt who supplied all the island's cranes up to the container age. This jetty was built in the late 1920s for the new railway mail boats coming into service, hence the name, which has remained to this day. The jetty now has a ro/ro ramp on each side. The ***Minerva II***, built by the G De Waal shipyard, at Zaltbommel was eventually broken up at Hendrik Ido Ambacht, south-east of Rotterdam, in late 1973.

(Derick Goubert)

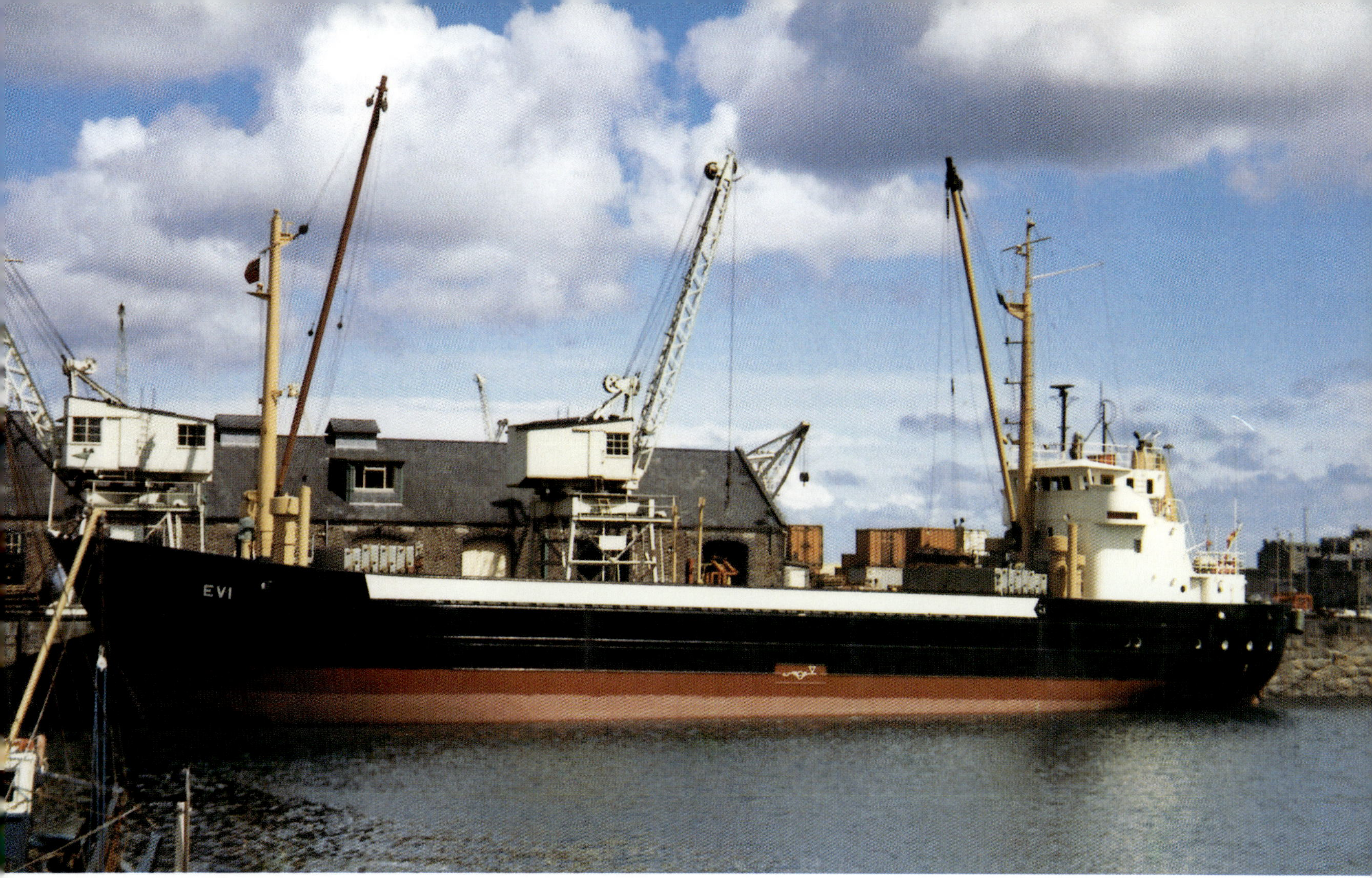

By contrast and looking very smart with a fresh coat of paint when moored at No. 8 berth, one of the few drying berths in St Peter Port harbour, is the ***Evi*** (DEU, 453grt/70) on charter to Huelin Shipping Services Ltd for its Portsmouth - Channel Islands route in the early 1970s. This berth was always used by the London boats until they moved to a deep water berth after about 1946. The ***Evi*** was one of a large group of similar shelterdeck coasters built for Dietrich Sander between 1968 and 1974. By the end of the decade they were being sold to owners all over the world. The ***Evi***, built at the J C Slob shipyard in Sliedrecht, sailed for a time under the Austrian flag as a cost-saving measure. She became ***Evi II*** in 1977 and then ***Isla Santa Fe*** and ***Evi I*** before becoming ***Valentina I*** on 29 February 1984 and then ***Tanja von Barssel*** on 4 April that same year. She traded only briefly under this name as she was lost in the eastern Mediterranean in July 1984 after having a fire in her engine room.

(Derick Goubert)

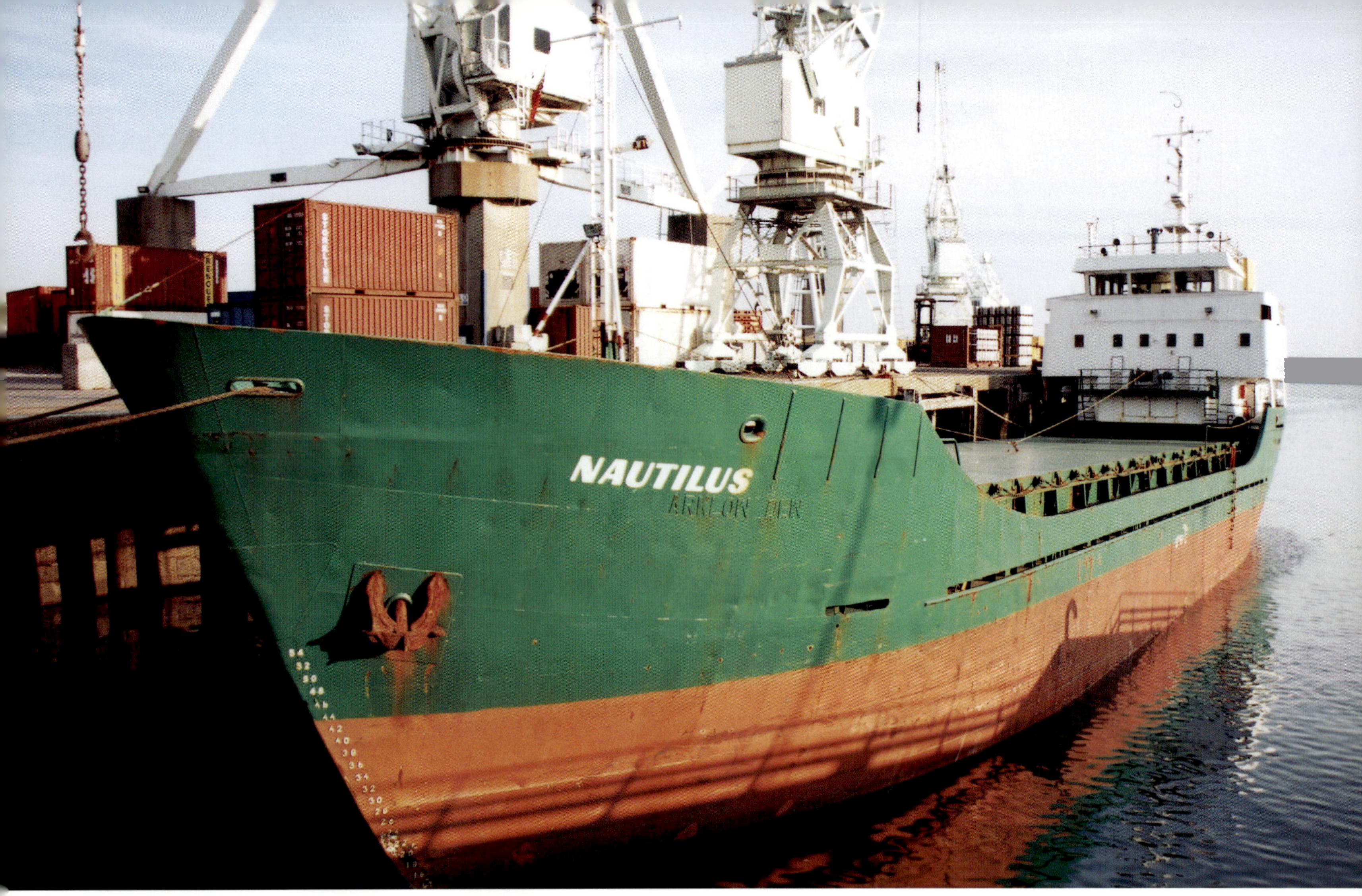

After arriving the previous day, the ***Nautilus*** (NIS, 1094gt/78) lies at No. 4 Berth in St Peter Port on a sunny 27 January 2000 after discharging a part-cargo of fertiliser from Porsgrunn, the balance having already been discharged at St Helier. The ship was built by Scheepswerf Bijholt at Foxhol as ***Terona***. In 1984, she joined the fleet of Arklow Shipping and was renamed ***Arklow View***, this being only slightly modified to ***Arklow Dew*** following sale in 1988. It was in 1994 that she became ***Nautilus*** when purchased by Norwegian owners. She was sold within Norway in 2000, her new owners transferring her to the Bahamas flag and renaming her ***Fritind***.

(Tony Rive)

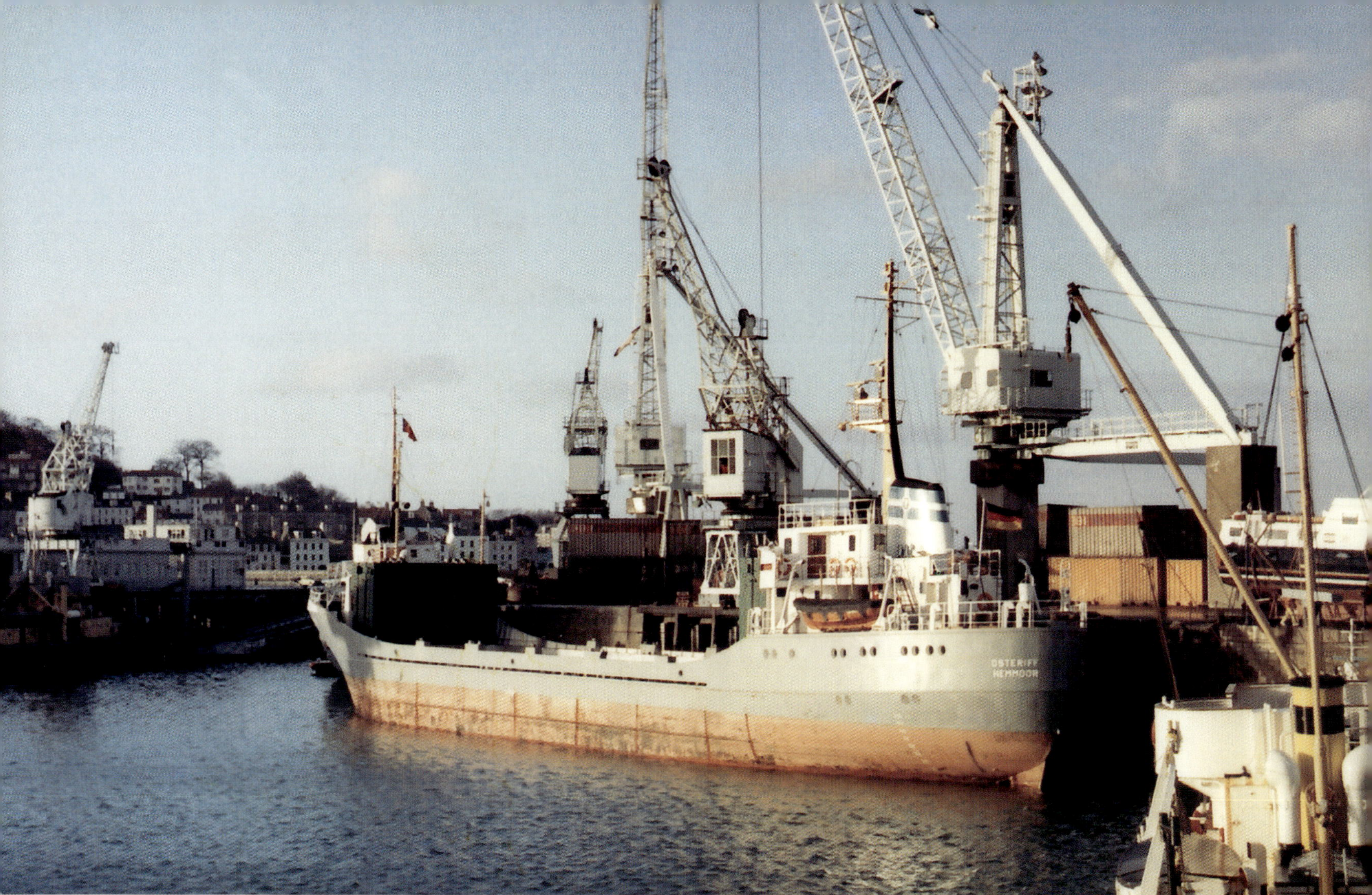

Discharging containers at No. 5 Berth in St Peter Port in the late afternoon is the ***Osteriff*** (DEU, 999grt/71), at the time on charter to Commodore Shipping. She is another product of the J J Sietas yard in Hamburg, being an example of the multipurpose Type 58 design. Later years saw her become ***Anette*** (1977), ***Renate*** (1986), ***Renate Omega*** (1987), ***Renate*** (1992) and ***Jenlil*** (1993). Just visible to the right is part of the ***Ile de Serk*** (GBR, 195grt/41), ex ***T.R.V. 2***, of the Isle of Sark Shipping Company Ltd. She was built at Rowhedge Ironworks, sold to operators in the West Indies in 1984, and lost in Hurricane "Hugo" in September 1988.

(Derick Goubert)

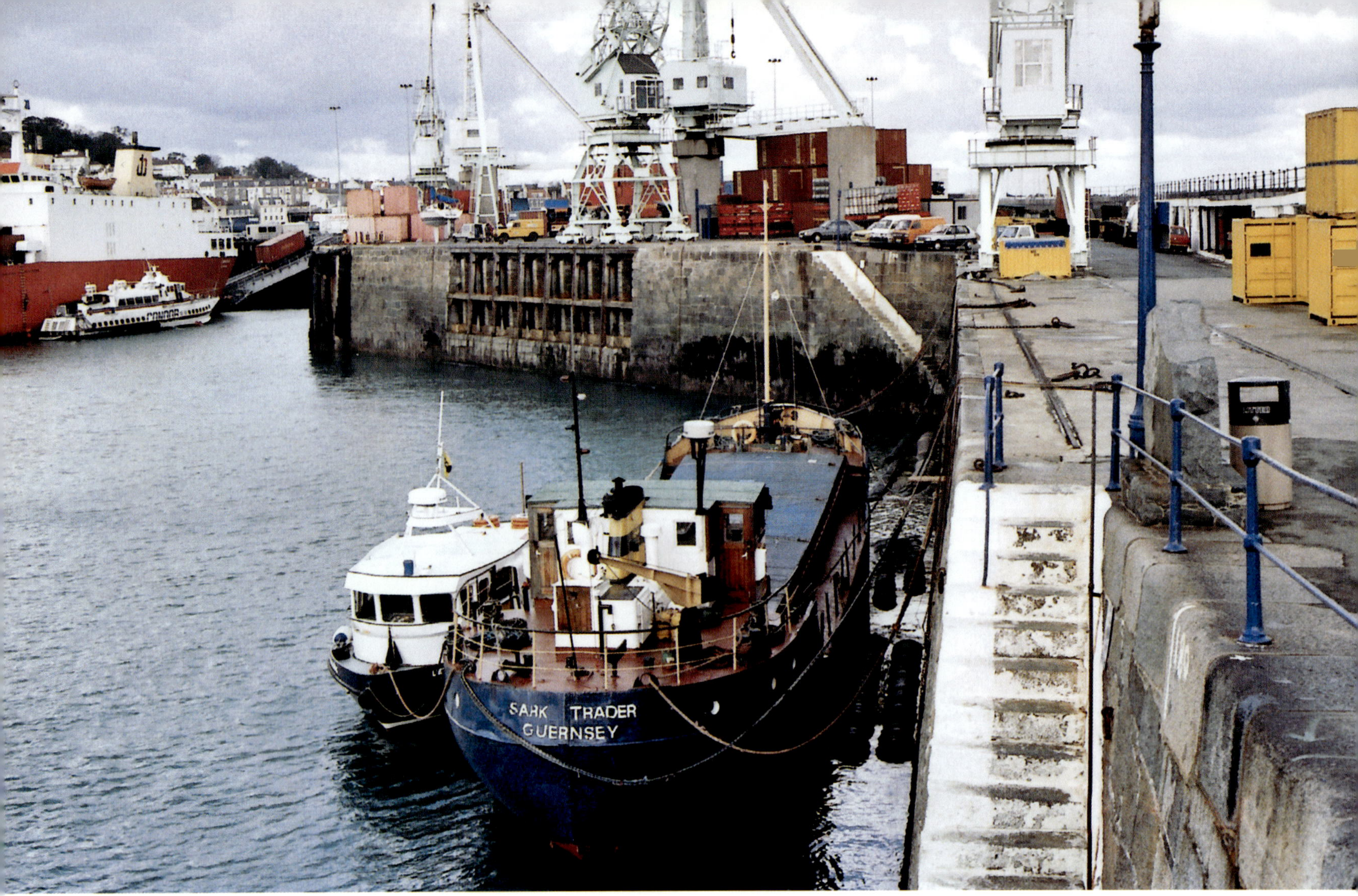

An off-season view, taken on 2 November 1990, of the ***Sark Trader*** (GBR, 212grt/63) and a passenger launch owned by the Isle of Sark Shipping Co Ltd to run supplies and passengers between St Peter Port and the smaller island of Sark. Built at the Gebr. Coops shipyard in Hoogezand as ***Function*** for the London & Rochester Trading Co Ltd, she attained notoriety in January 1978 when she found herself embarrassingly high and dry on top of the harbour wall at Wells-next-the-Sea following a very high spring tide, and she had to be lifted back into the water by mobile crane. She came to Sark in 1983 and was sold to a salmon farm in the early 1990s.

(Dave Hocquard)

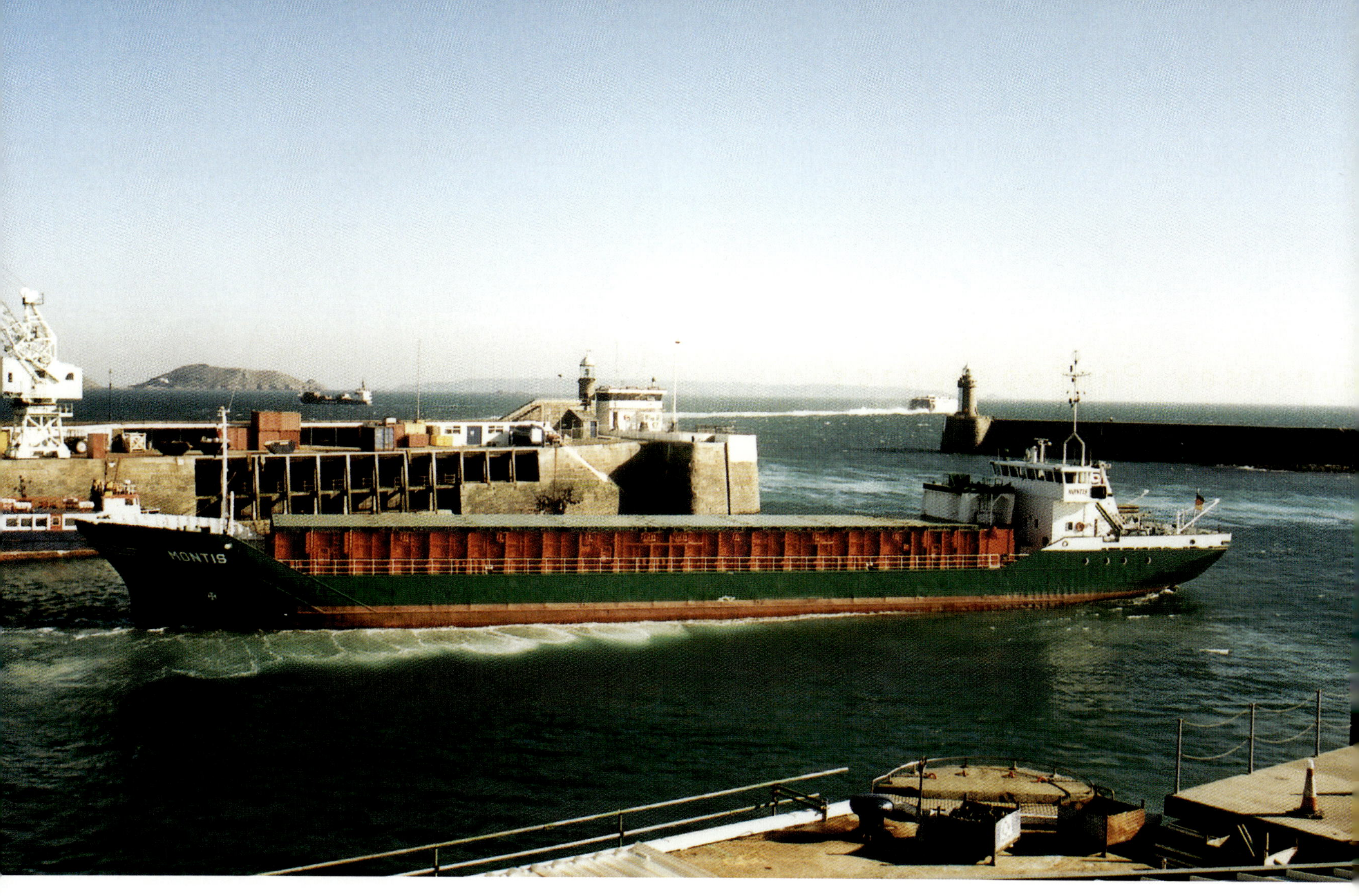

A busy scene in St Peter Port on a cloudless but breezy late afternoon of 7 November 2003 with the ***Montis*** (DEU, 1649gt/85) backing away from Berth 5 having discharged a part cargo of timber. In the background, the ***Huelin Dispatch*** is bound for Portsmouth having just left Berth 4 and the fast ferry ***Condor Express*** (BHS, 5005gt/96) has just vacated Berth 3 and is bound to Jersey. The islands of Jethou and Sark are in the far distance. This coaster is another product of the Hugo Peters yard in Wewelsfleth and was named ***Premiere*** until 2002.

(Peter Stewart)

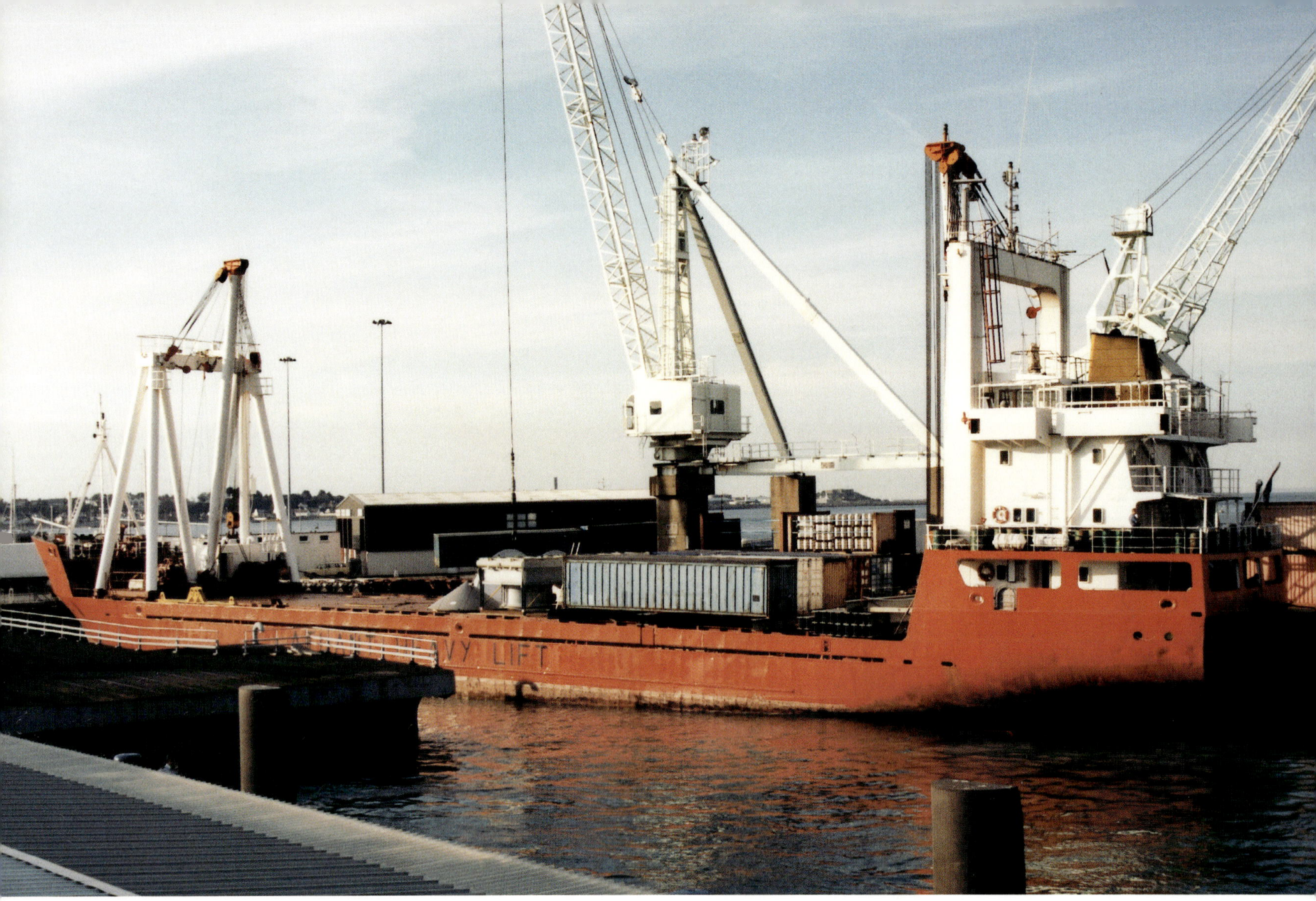

An unusal visitor to St Peter Port's No. 4 Berth on 7 July 1997 was the heavy-lift ship ***Plitvice*** (HRV, 2044gt/79). She had arrived from Dordrecht with a gas turbine for the island's electricity generating station. The vessel was built at the De Waal ship yard in Zaltbommel as ***Elger***, her change of name coming in 1985. In 2002, she was sold to operators in Georgia and was renamed ***Lewis***.

(Peter Stewart)

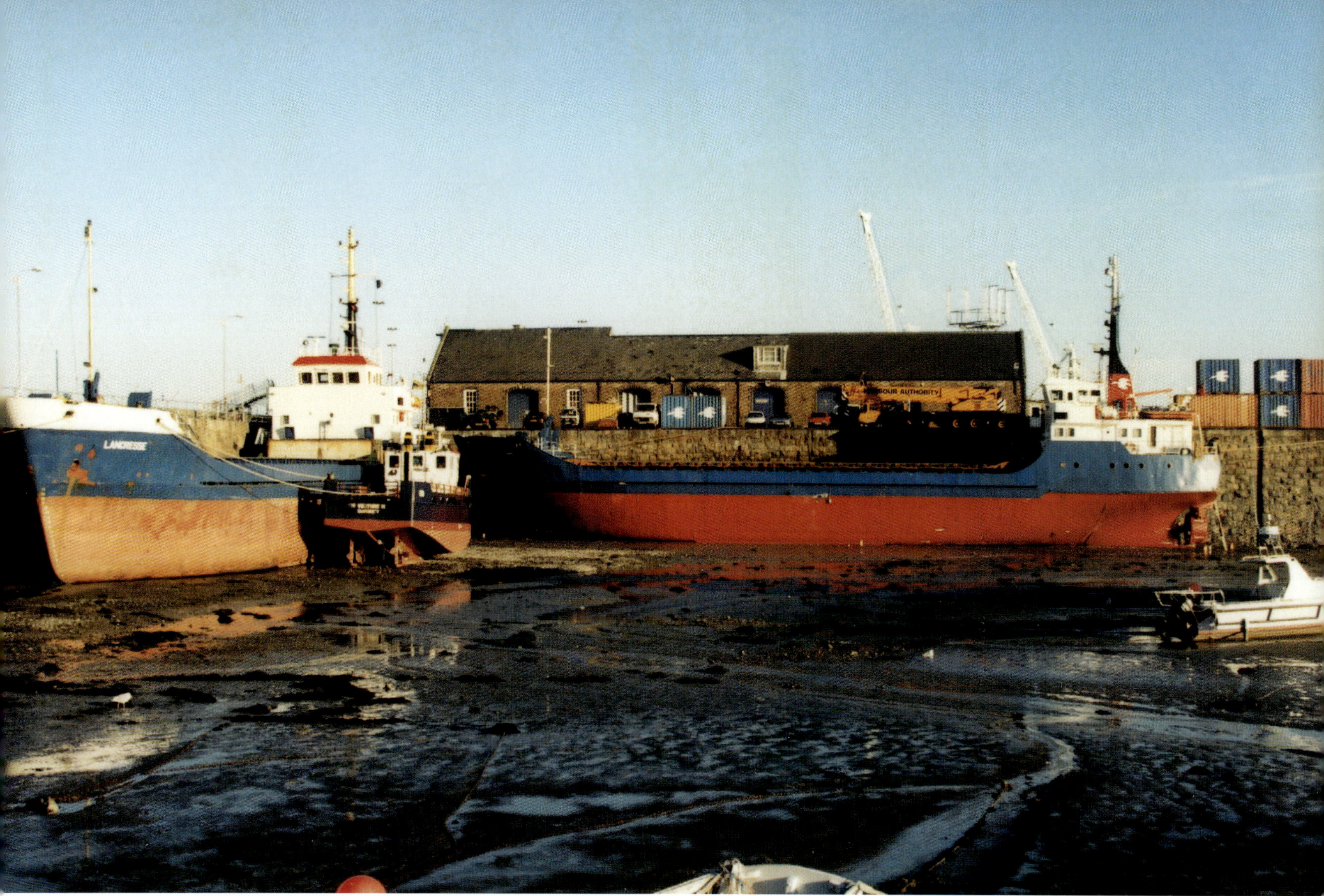

Over the Christmas and New Year period, it is usually possible to see vessels in the Alderney Shipping fleet as they lay by in St Peter Port. Noted together on a sunny day in late December 1996 are the sisterships ***Isis*** and ***Lancresse*** (674gt/78), ex ***Bressay Sound***-94, ***Edgar Dorman***-89, both built at the Jadewerft shipyard in Wilhelmshaven. Operated by Alderney Shipping, ownership is actually in the hands of Allied Coasters Ltd. This is our first view of the latter vessel which was renamed ***Burhou I*** in 1997.

(Tony Rive)

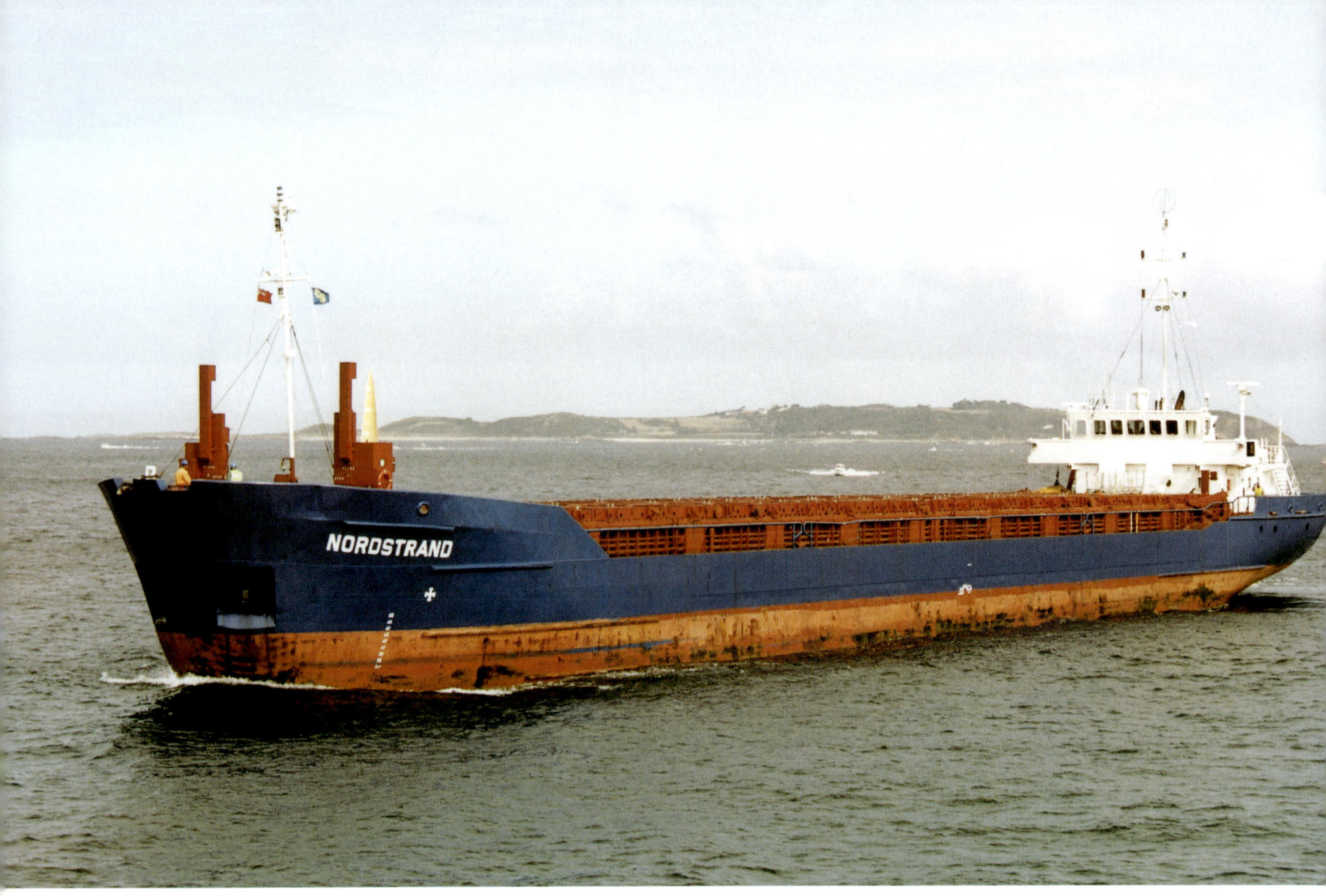

The ***Huelin Dispatch*** has been an ideal vessel for the Channel Islands service and she has also proved to be very reliable. However, she is occasionally off service for scheduled overhaul and her usual replacement is the ***Nordstrand*** (BRB, 1970gt/91), ex ***Nicole***-93, built at the Damen shipyard in Gorinchem. She was photographed as she approached St Peter Port on 27 August 2000, almost at the end of a two-week charter when she replaced the ***Huelin Dispatch***.

(Peter Stewart)

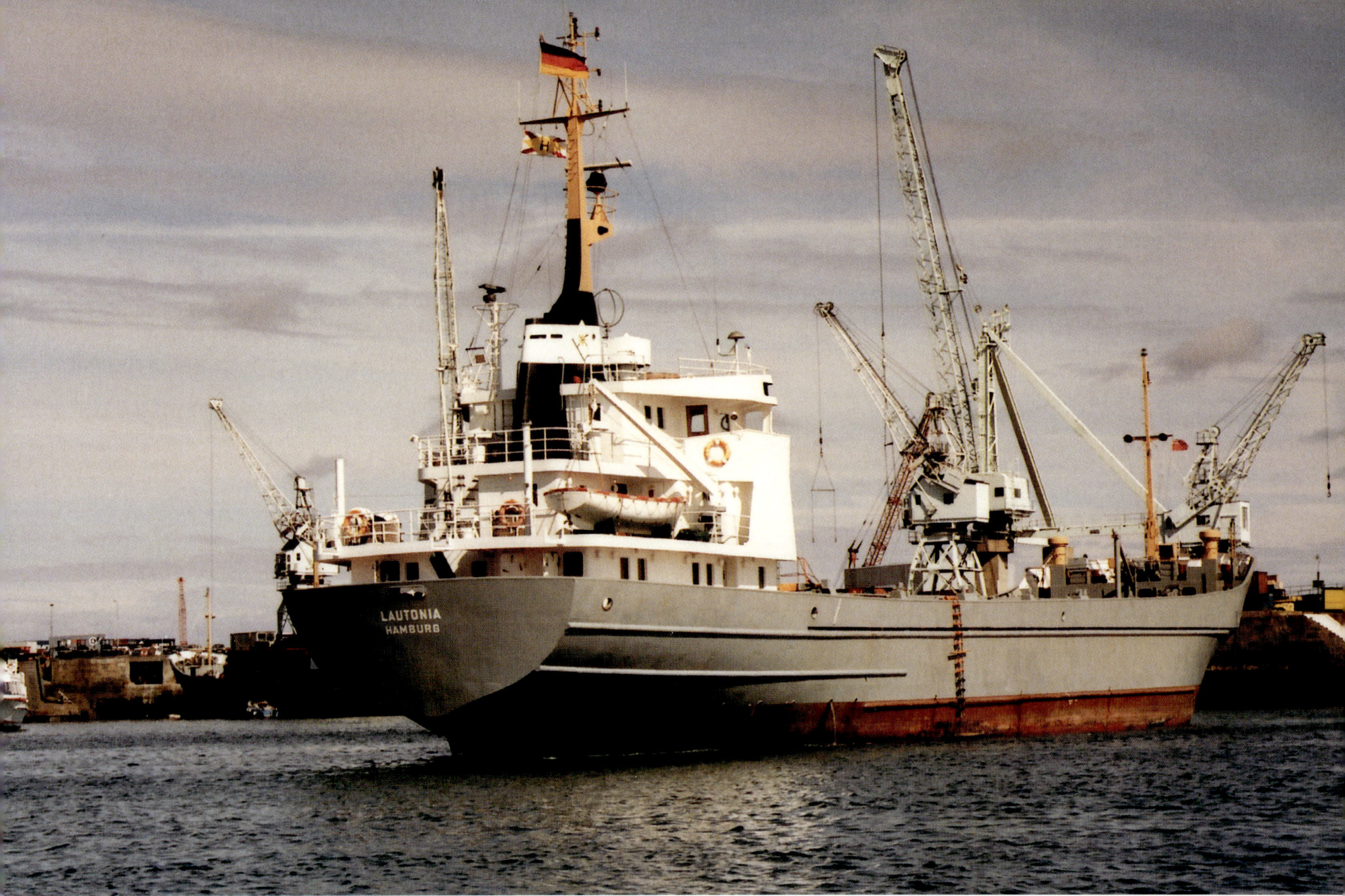

Backing away from No 6 berth in St Peter Port on the pleasantly sunny morning of 1 September 1986 is the Hamburg-registered ***Lautonia*** (DEU, 499grt/71) on charter to Huelin Shipping Services Ltd for its Portsmouth - Channel Islands container service. She is wearing Huelin's funnel colours of the time; the house flag is the same as today minus the R. The ***Lautonia***, ex ***Heinrich Knüppel***-85, was a product of the Husumer Schiffswerf in Husum and equipped to carry 136 TEU; she had a service speed of 13 knots. In 1989, she was sold and renamed ***Mercator***, becoming ***Mercator I*** in 2000.

(Dave Hocquard)

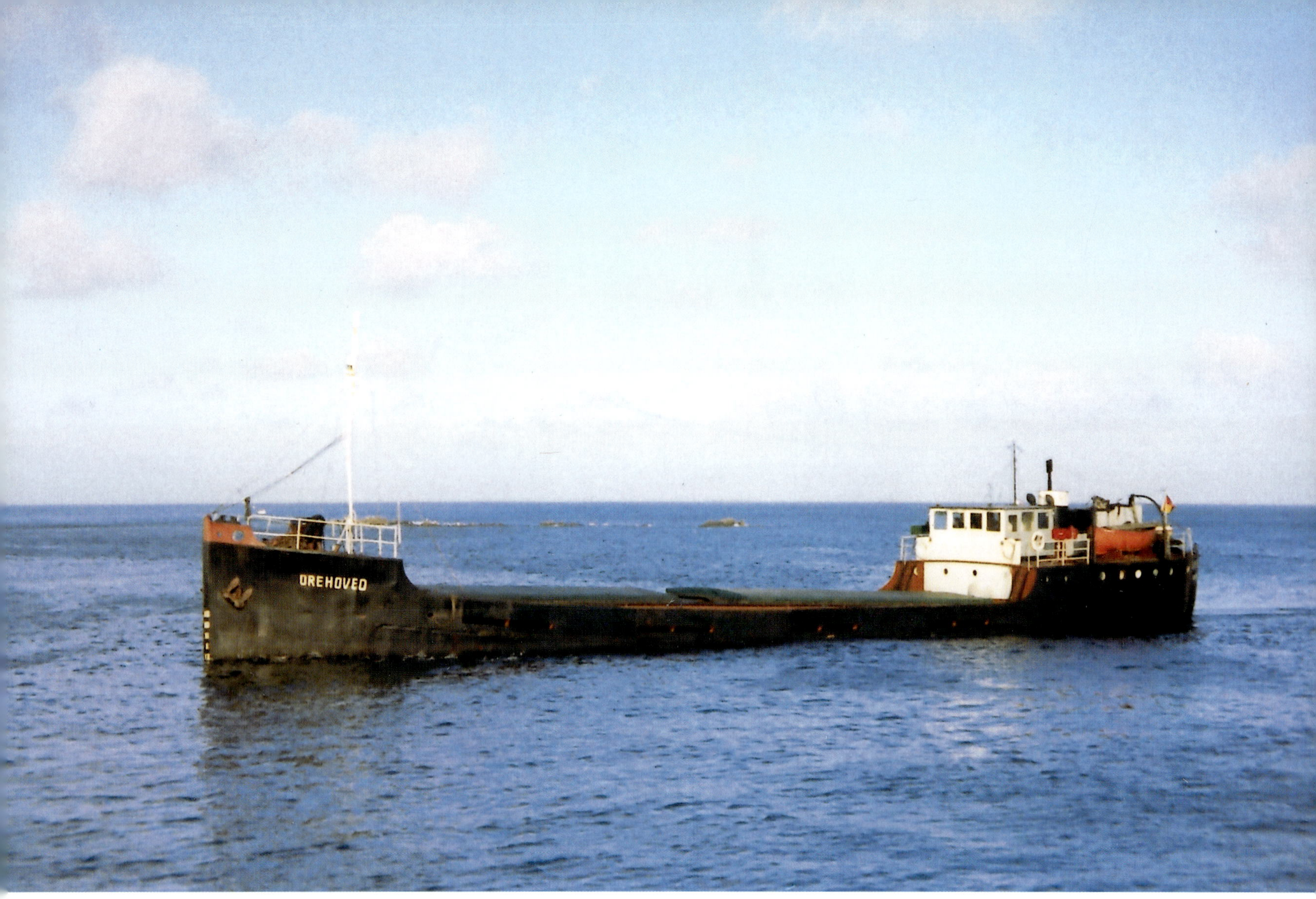

From the Guernsey's capital, we now move to the island's other port, St Sampson's. Seen approaching St Sampson's Harbour in the early 1970s is the ***Orehoved*** (DEU, 310grt/35) built by Goole Shipbuilding & Repair Co Ltd. It is rare to see a British-built coaster under the German flag as she was from 1968 to 1972. This little coaster had as many as 10 different names and 12 owners from 1935 to 1993 when she was deleted from *Lloyd's Register*.

(Derick Goubert)

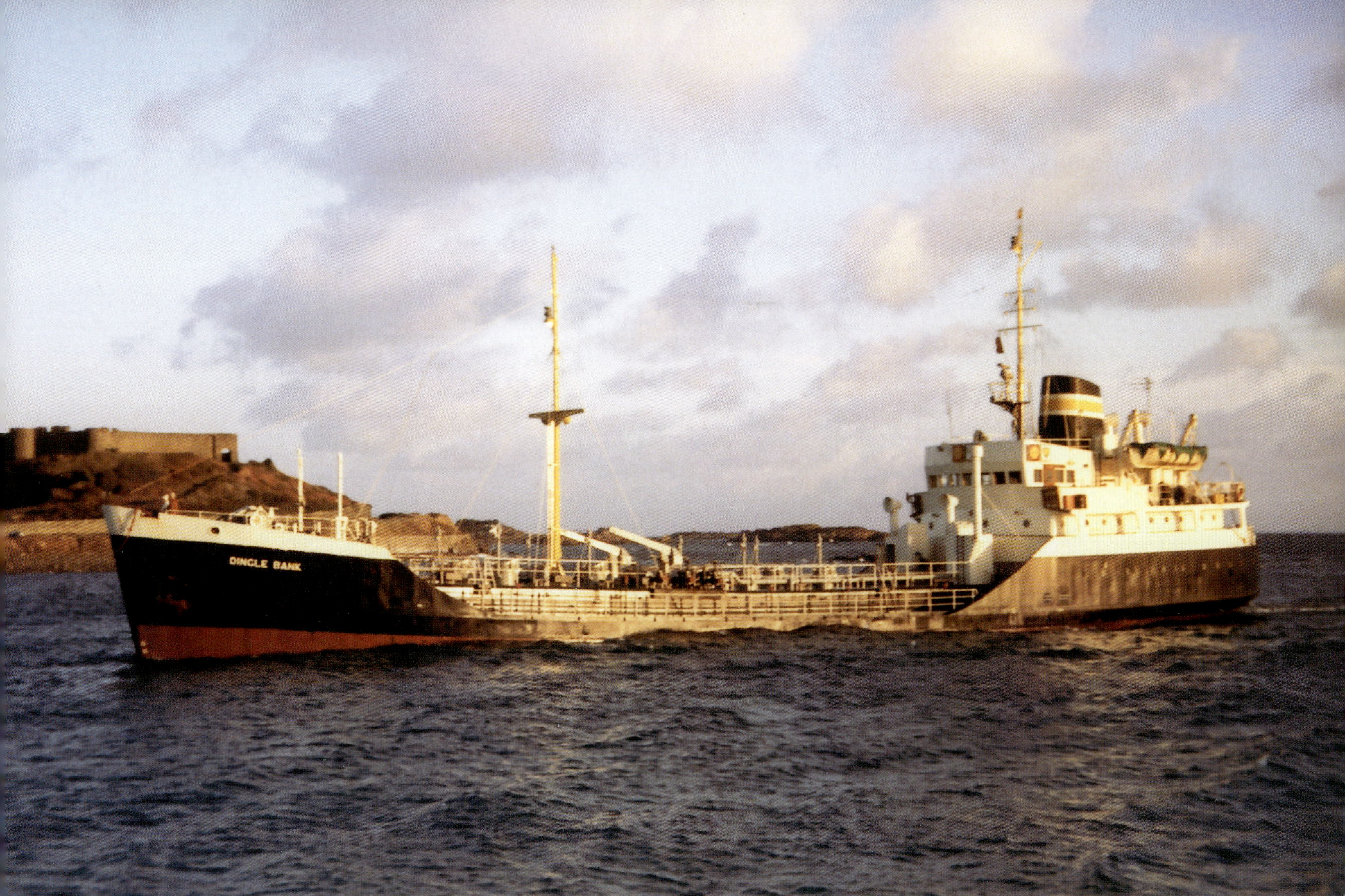

With Vale Castle prominent on the hill in the background, the Shell tanker ***Dingle Bank*** (GBR, 1177grt/66) cautiously approaches the entrance to St Sampson's Harbour in the winter sunshine. A lot of care is needed when entering St Sampson's due to the strong current which runs up and down the coast just off shore. This tanker, built by Grangemouth Dockyard, was renamed ***Shell Engineer*** in 1979 then sold abroad in 1990 to Maltese flag owners before going to Nigeria as ***Hensmor Agro Allide*** in 1998 in the ownership of Hensmor Nigeria Ltd.

(Derick Goubert)

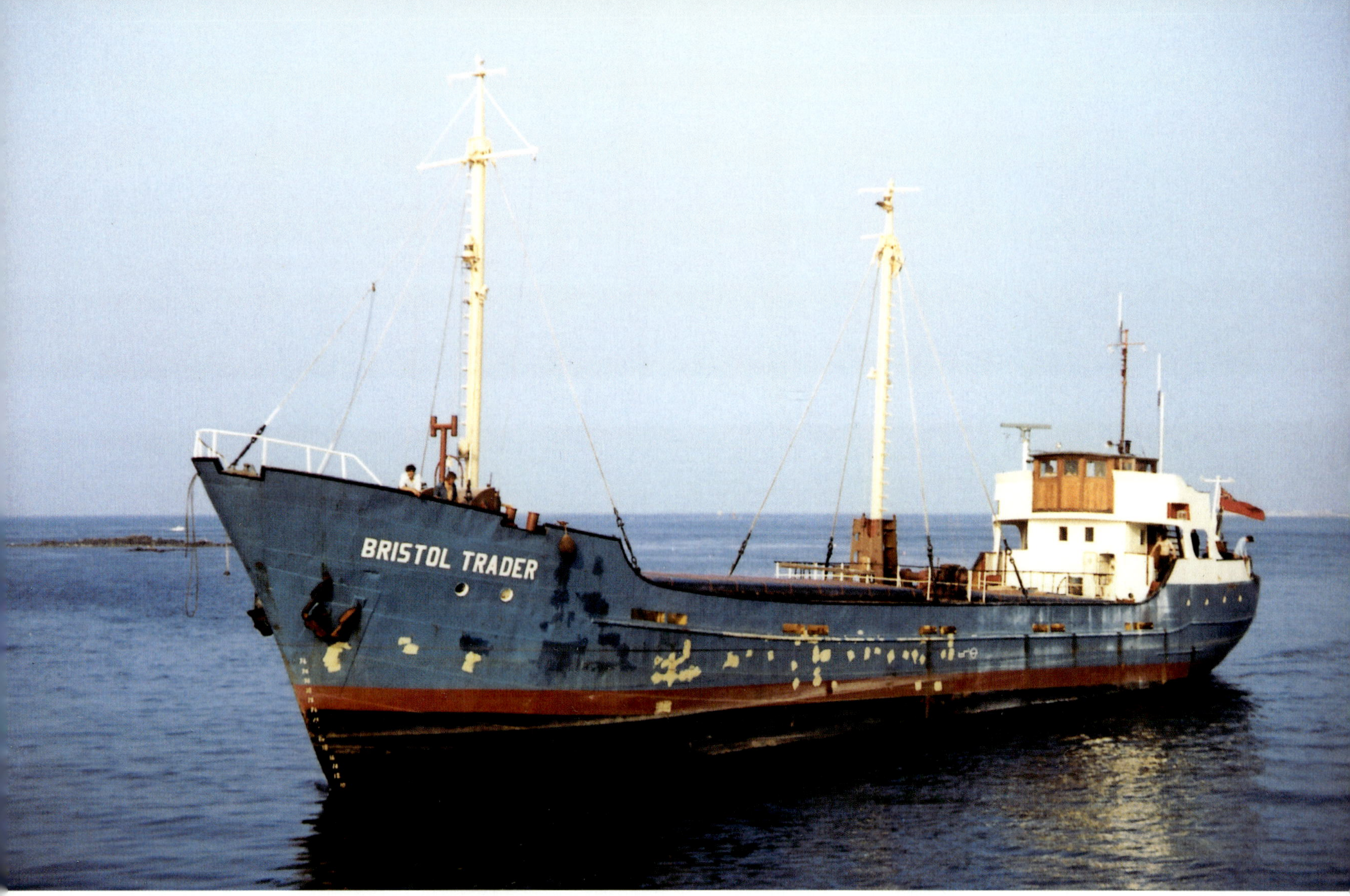

The ***Bristol Trader*** (GBR, 400grt/51), built at the Fr. Lürssen shipyard in Bremen, enters her home port of St Sampson's. She was registered in Guernsey from 1972 until she arrived at Bloors Wharf, Rainham, Kent, on 25 January 1979 to be broken up. During this time she had four different owners. The photograph is undated so the owners are not known. She was built as ***Milos*** for J W C Kampen, of Bremen, and was lengthened in 1955 by 9,00 metres. Having had a serious fire in her accommodation in Bristol Docks in 1969, she was then declared a constructive total loss. In 1970 she was sold to Gemini Ships (UK) Ltd and repaired.

(Derick Goubert)

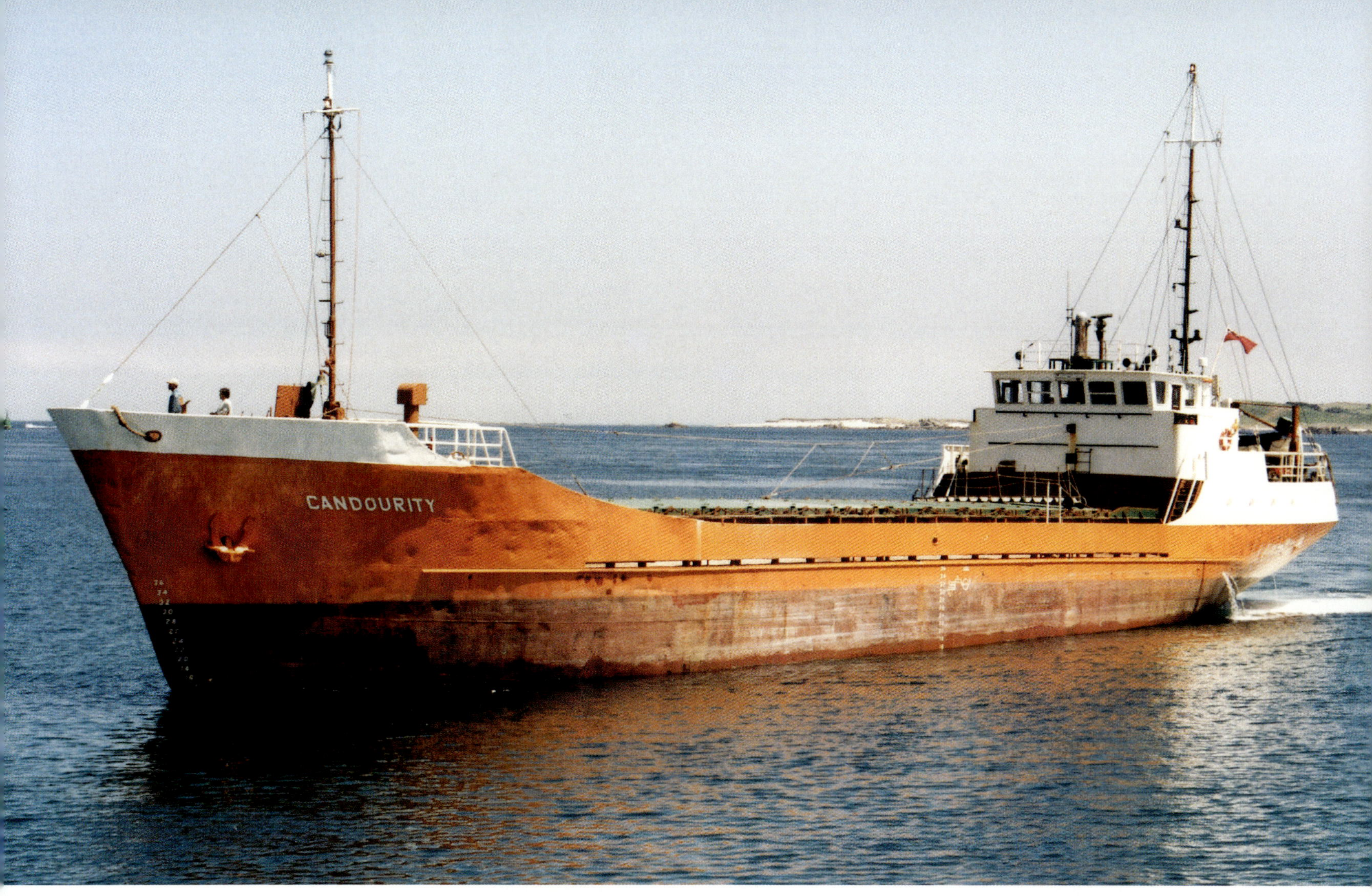

In addition to being a lifelong enthusiast of coastal shipping, as testified by the credits to several of the photographs in this book, Derick Goubert has also been the owner and Master of several vessels. Approaching St Sampson's Harbour on a sunny 23 June 1999 is his ***Candourity*** (GBR, 559gt/75), the early summer sun highlighting her "Goubert orange" hull. She was inbound from La Pallice in ballast and she was putting in to her home port for water and supplies sailing on the same tide for Rotterdam. The ***Candourity*** was one of four sisterships built at Foxhol in the mid-1970s for F T Everard & Sons Ltd. She was sold to Derick in November 1992 and remained in his ownership until sold to Queen Makoua Charlotte of Douala (Cameroun) in August 2002 and renamed ***Makoua Express***.

(Peter Stewart)

Another product of the Lürssen yard in Bremen, the small German coaster ***Crail*** (DEU, 299grt/49) unloading sand at St Sampson's in the early 1970s is a reminder of how small coasters used to be. By this time she had already been lengthened from 31,18m to 41,52m. When the photo was taken she was owned by Violet & Derek Borstel of Duisburg. She later passed to several British owners under the Panama flag but did little trading and spent some time laid up in London's Royal Docks. Sold to Panamanian-flag owners in 1980, she was renamed ***Northern Venture***, becoming ***Jasibo*** in 1981 and ***Sibo*** in 1982. She is thought to have been demolished some twenty years later.

(Derick Goubert)

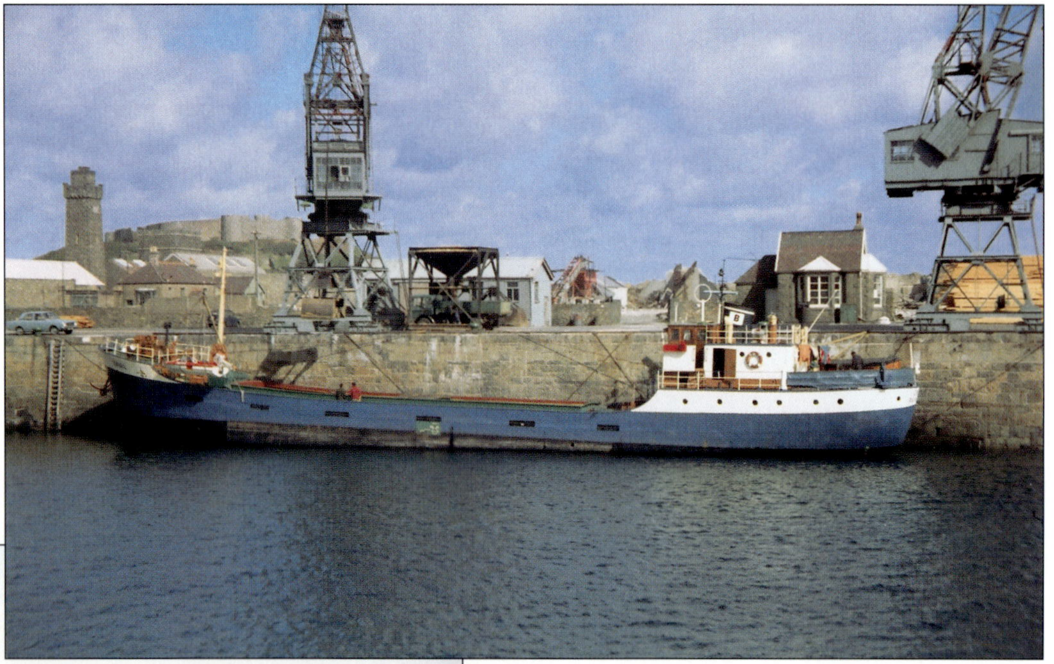

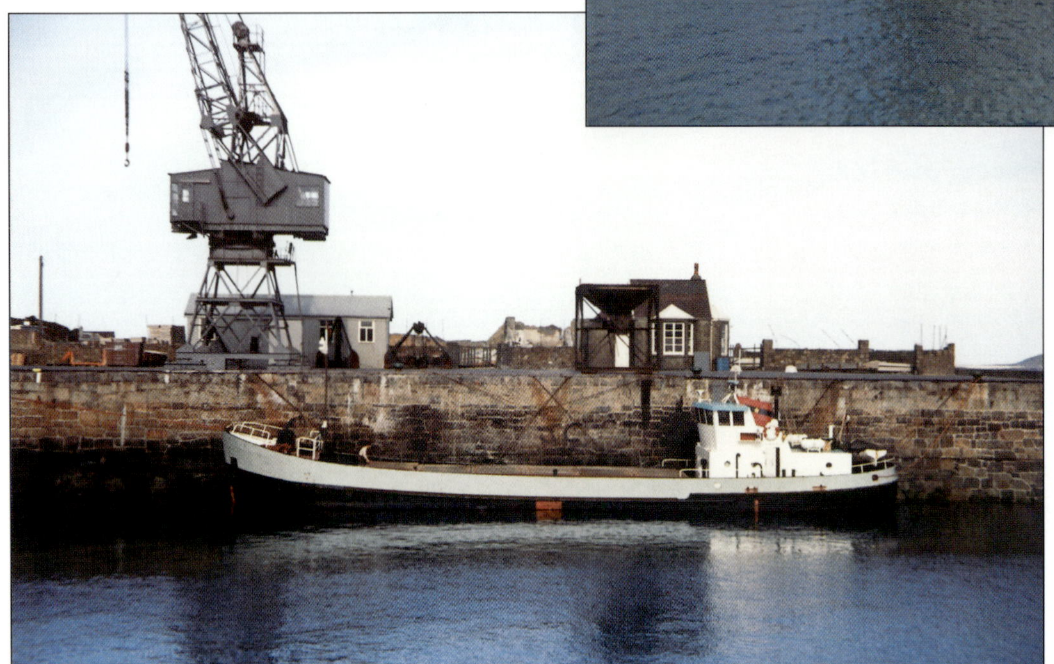

Seen at St Sampson's shortly before her loss, the diminutive ***Hooness*** (GBR, 196grt/65), together with her sistership ***Edward Stone***, were the first coasters built for R Lapthorn & Co Ltd, of Hoo, and built at the Wivenhoe shipyard of James W Cook & Co. Both were regular traders to the Channel Islands. Sadly the ***Hooness*** was overwhelmed and foundered in heavy seas some 35 miles north-east of Barfleur during a voyage London to St Sampson's with a full cargo of bagged cement. All her crew were saved.

(Derick Goubert)

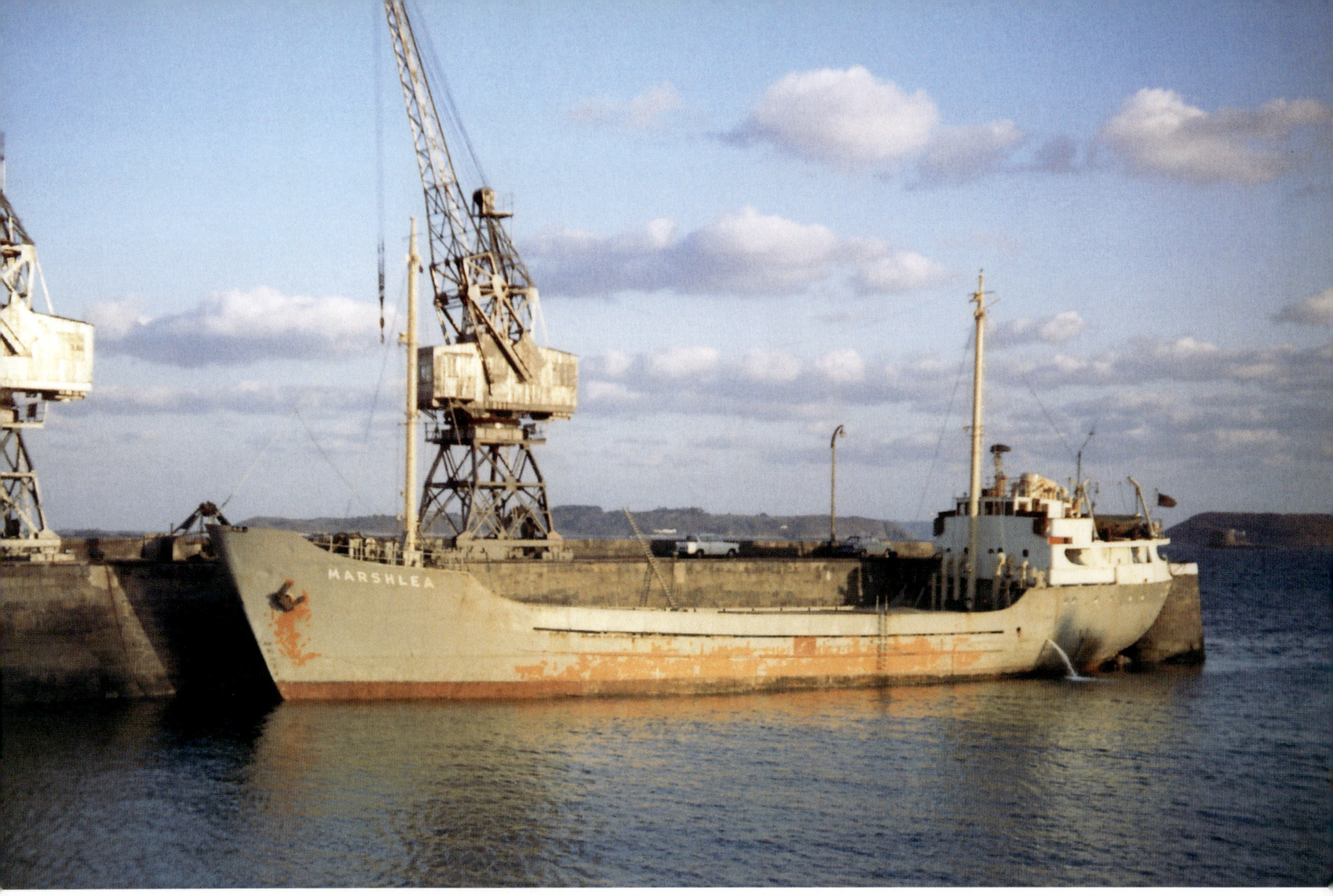

Another coaster to have served the Channel Islands over a long period was the ***Marshlea*** (GBR, 495grt/57). Originally she brought bagged cement from Northfleet and returned with stone from Ronez Quarry, Jersey, or St Sampson's, Guernsey, where we see her bathed in the evening sunshine in the late 1960s when still owned by Hindlea Shipping Co Ltd, of Cardiff. Following conversion into a bulk cement carrier in 1978, all her return voyages were in ballast. She was built speculatively at the Kalmar shipyard in Sweden and was broken up in Holland in 1982.

(Derick Goubert)

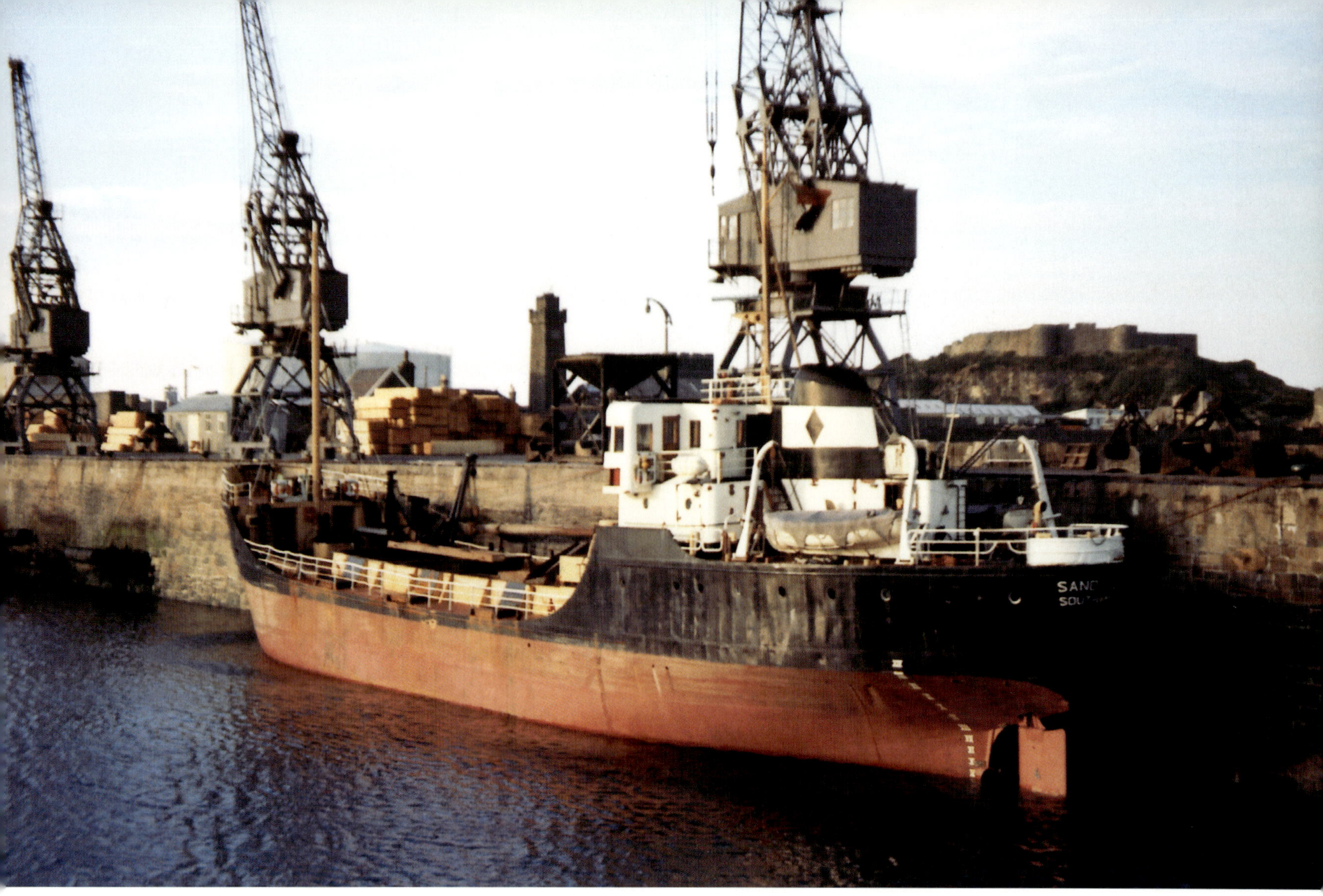

For many years sand has had to be imported into Guernsey for the building trades normally in dry cargo coasters, but occasionally in sand dredgers. Here we see the ***Sand Gull*** (GBR, 534gt/69), built by J Bolson & Son Ltd, Poole, and owned by South Coast Shipping Ltd, of Southampton. She was broken up in late 1992 at Marchwood near Southampton after grounding near Ventnor (Isle of Wight). Above her stern is Vale Castle, built to guard the entrance to St Sampson's Harbour against attack mainly during troubles with France.

(Derick Goubert)

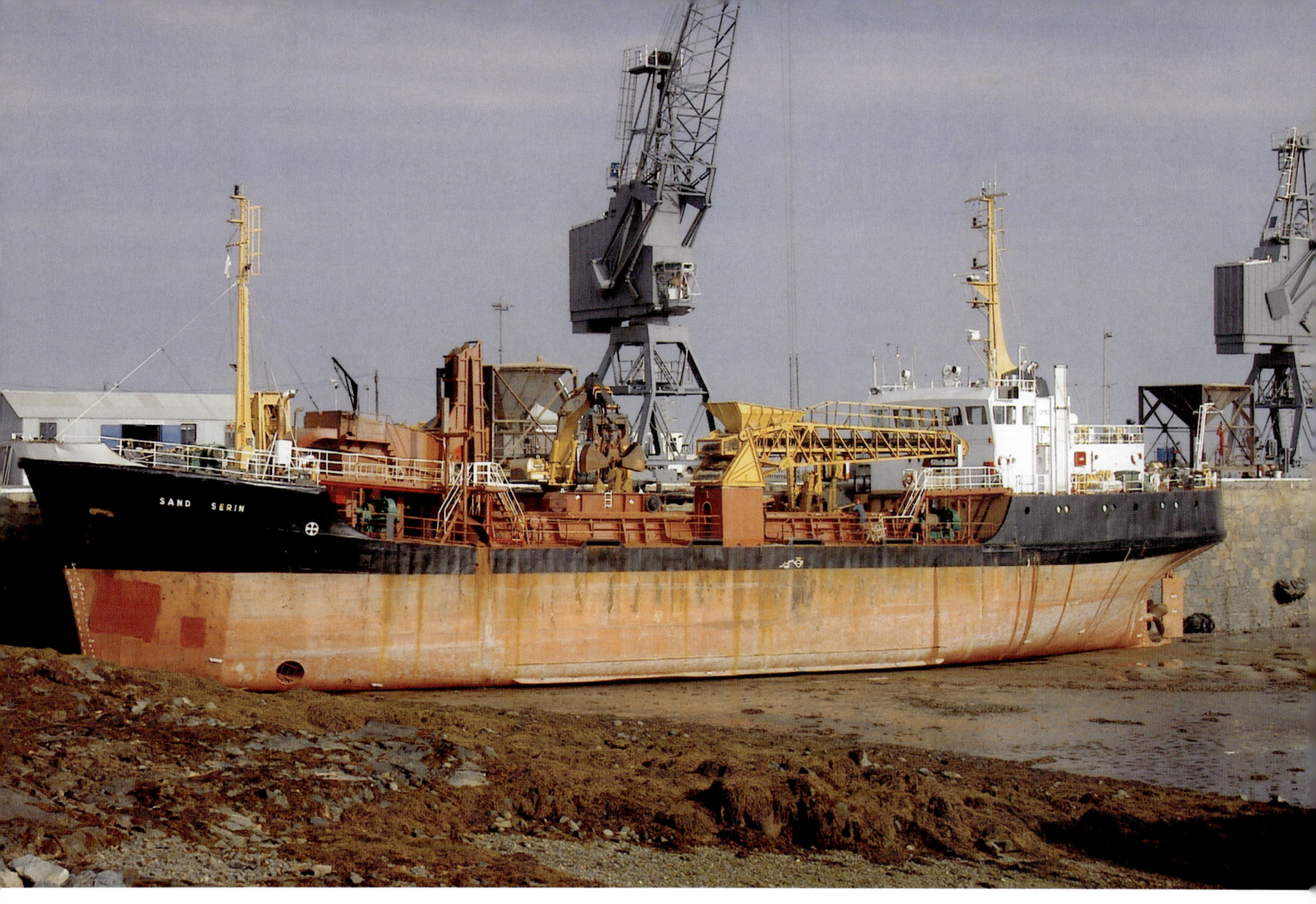

Exemplifying a more modern design of sand dredger is the ***Sand Serin*** (GBR, 1283gt/74), built by Clelands Shipbuilding Co Ltd at Wallsend on the River Tyne. Registered at Southampton, she is usually to be found working in the Solent but on a sunny 12 September 2006 she was noted discharging her cargo in St Sampson's.

(Tony Rive)

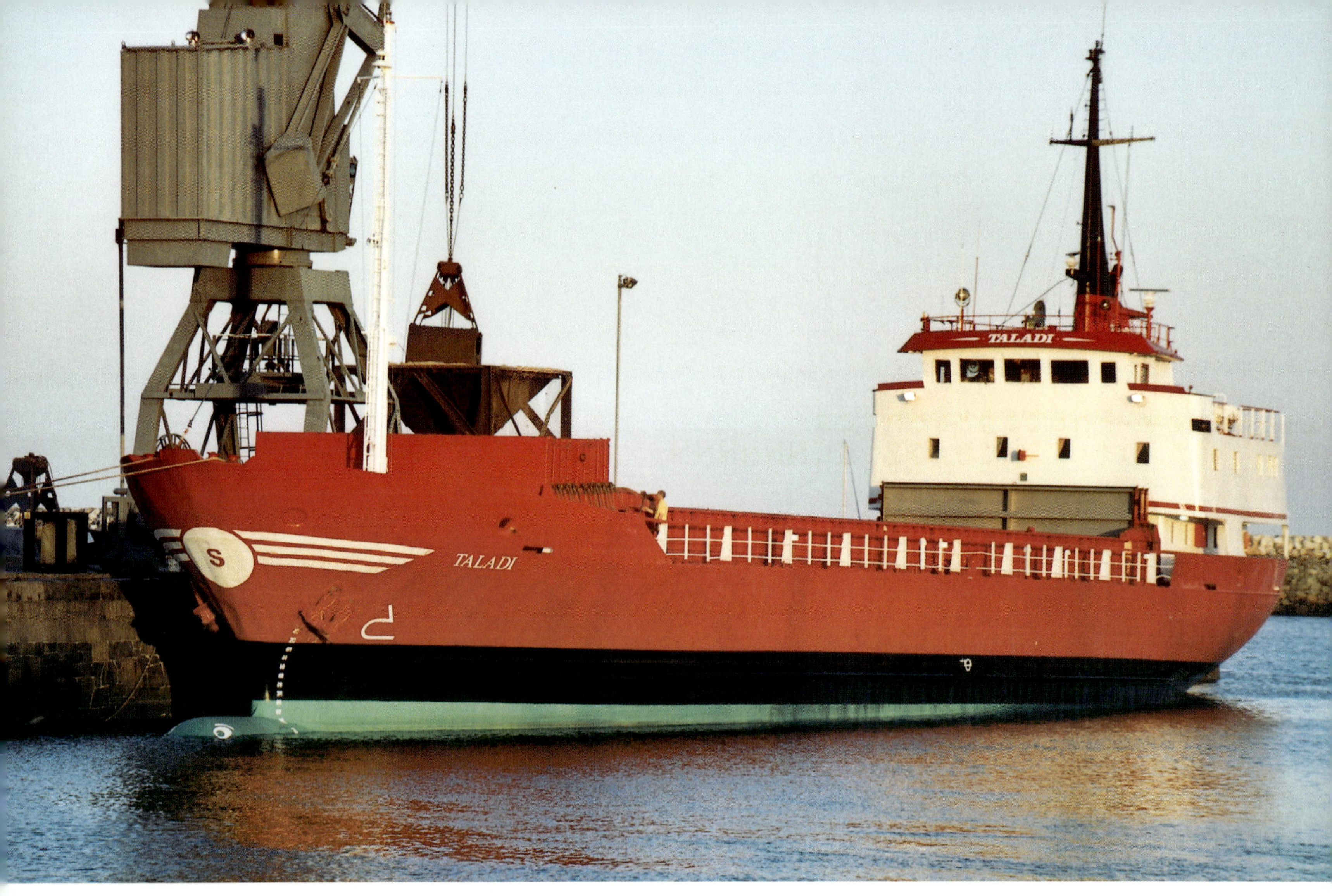

An elderly but immaculate ***Taladi*** (DIS, 1106gt/71) discharges a part cargo of Leca from the Danish port of Randers on 28 June 2002. She had already called at Jersey to discharge 500 tons, the remaining 400 tons was for Guernsey. She sailed the next day in ballast for Hamburg. Note the eyes painted on her bulbous bow. Owned by Taladi Aps of Frederikshavn since 1993, she had four previous names ***Sonja Hove*** until 1993, ***Stevnsland*** until 1983, ***Mor-Sines*** until 1976, and initially ***Ruth Klint*** until 72. Following the sudden death of her captain/owner, she was laid up at Frederikshavn and Svendborg in early 2006 and was later bought by Danish operators and renamed ***Valborg***.

(Peter Stewart)

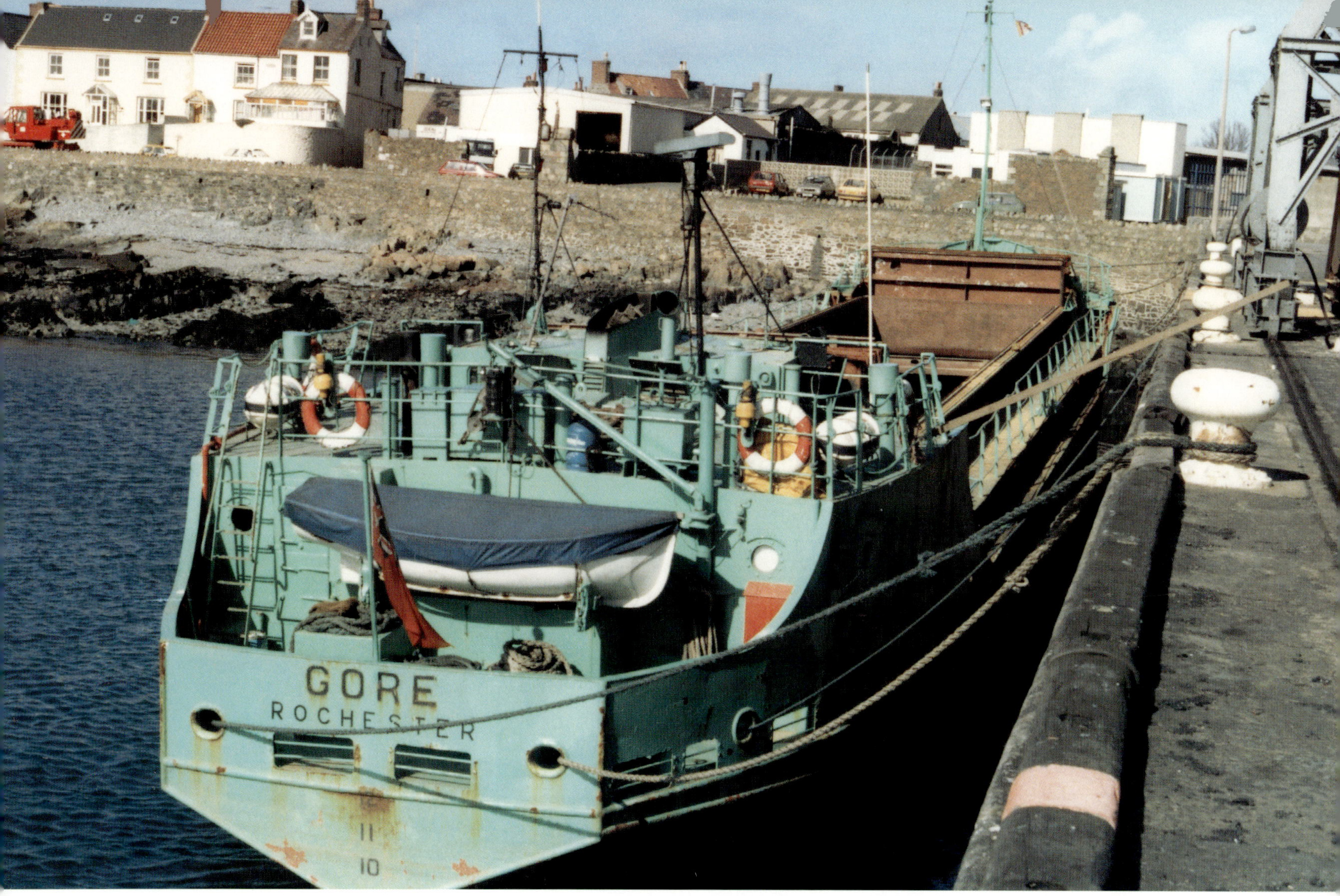

One of the oddest coloured coasters seen in the islands was the Rochester-registered ***Gore*** (GBR, 392grt/69) owned by Brian T Cuckow and seen here at Northside St Sampson's in the late 1980s. She was built at Selby by Cochrane & Sons Ltd as ***Eloquence*** for the London & Rochester Trading Co Ltd (Crescent Shipping Ltd), also of Rochester. After being rebuilt during 1998 for J J Prior (Transport) Ltd and renamed ***Peter Prior***, she entered the sand trade from Fingringhoe (Essex) to the River Thames and is still in this service today.

(the late Peter Leadbeater)

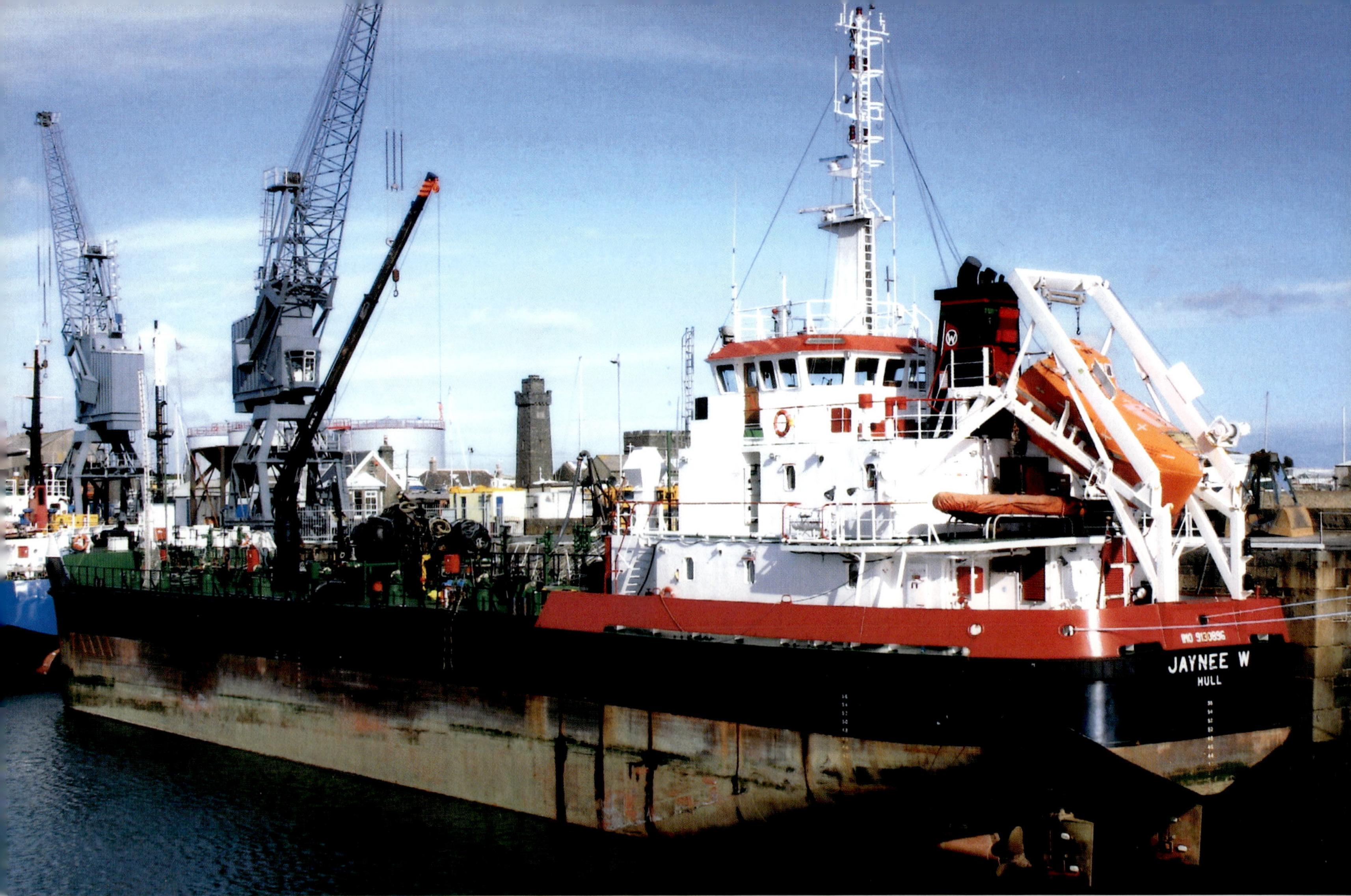

The ***Jaynee W*** (GBR, 1689gt/96) is owned by J Whitaker (Tankers) Ltd, based in Hull. Having arrived from Fawley with heavy oil for the island's power station on 30 October 2005, she is discharging her cargo at the outer berth on the North side of St Sampson's into the power station's tanks further up the harbour. Built by Yorkshire Drydock Co Ltd in Hull, she was the first new tanker in the Whitaker fleet and was designed mainly for bunkering larger ships around the Southampton and Solent area. This explains the large fenders on her tank deck and also the hydraulic crane for handling the bunkering hoses.

(Peter Stewart)

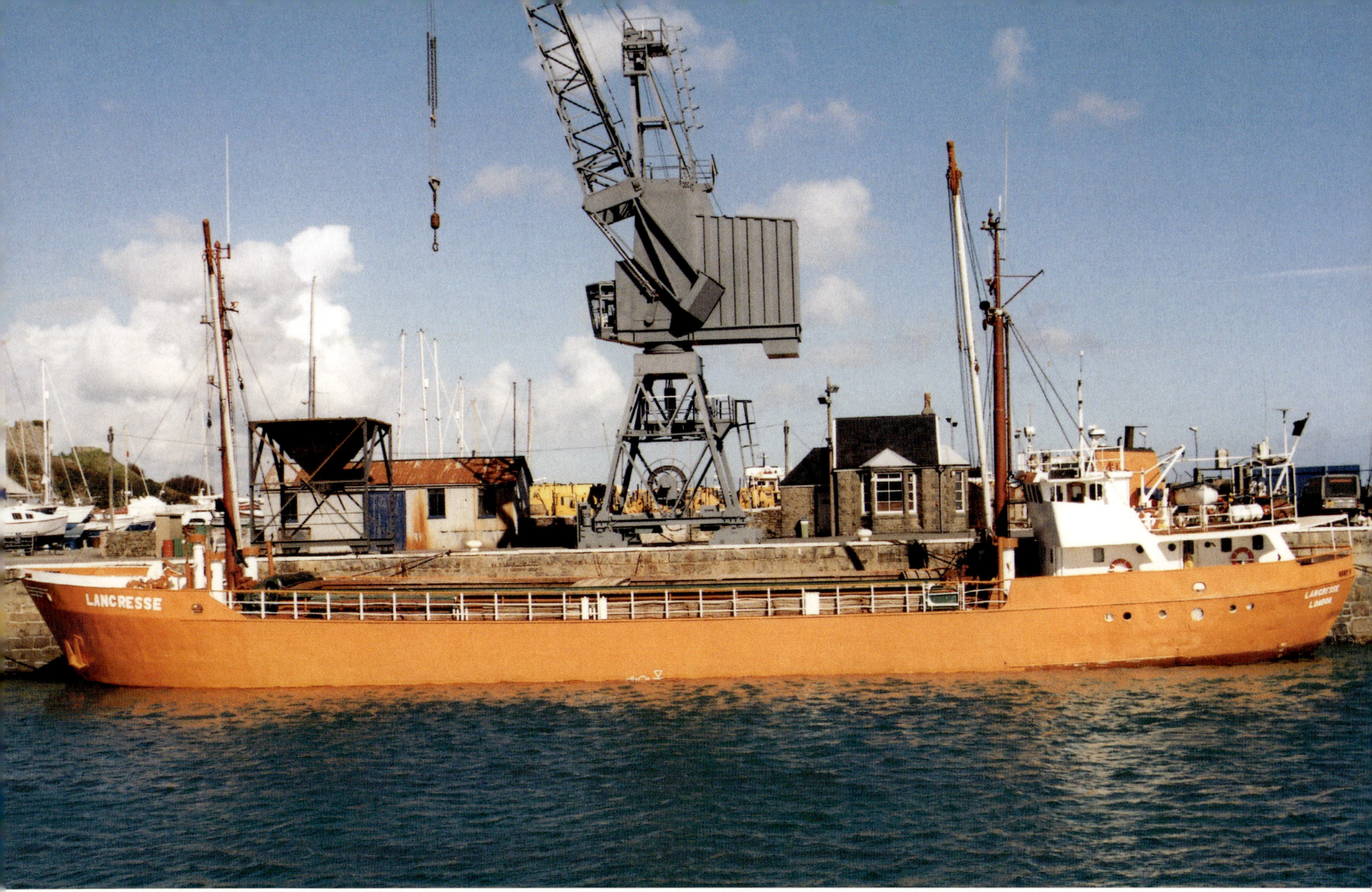

The bright orange hull leaves us little doubt that the ***Lancresse*** (GBR, 534gt/75), photographed on 5 April 1998, is one of Derick Goubert's coasters. She is an example of a hugely successful standard design of coaster built at the Nordsøværftet shipyard in Ringkøbing. Under her original name of ***Platessa***, she traded worldwide like many of her sisterships and was frequently noted carrying explosives to the West Indies. A sale within Denmark in 1991 saw her renamed ***Trobørg*** and she was sold on to become ***Jenstar*** in 1995. Two years later she was bought by Derick Goubert but her design was not really suitable for coastal trading around the UK and to the near-continent. Consequently she was sold to Faroese owners and renamed ***Skurin*** in 1999.

(Peter Stewart)

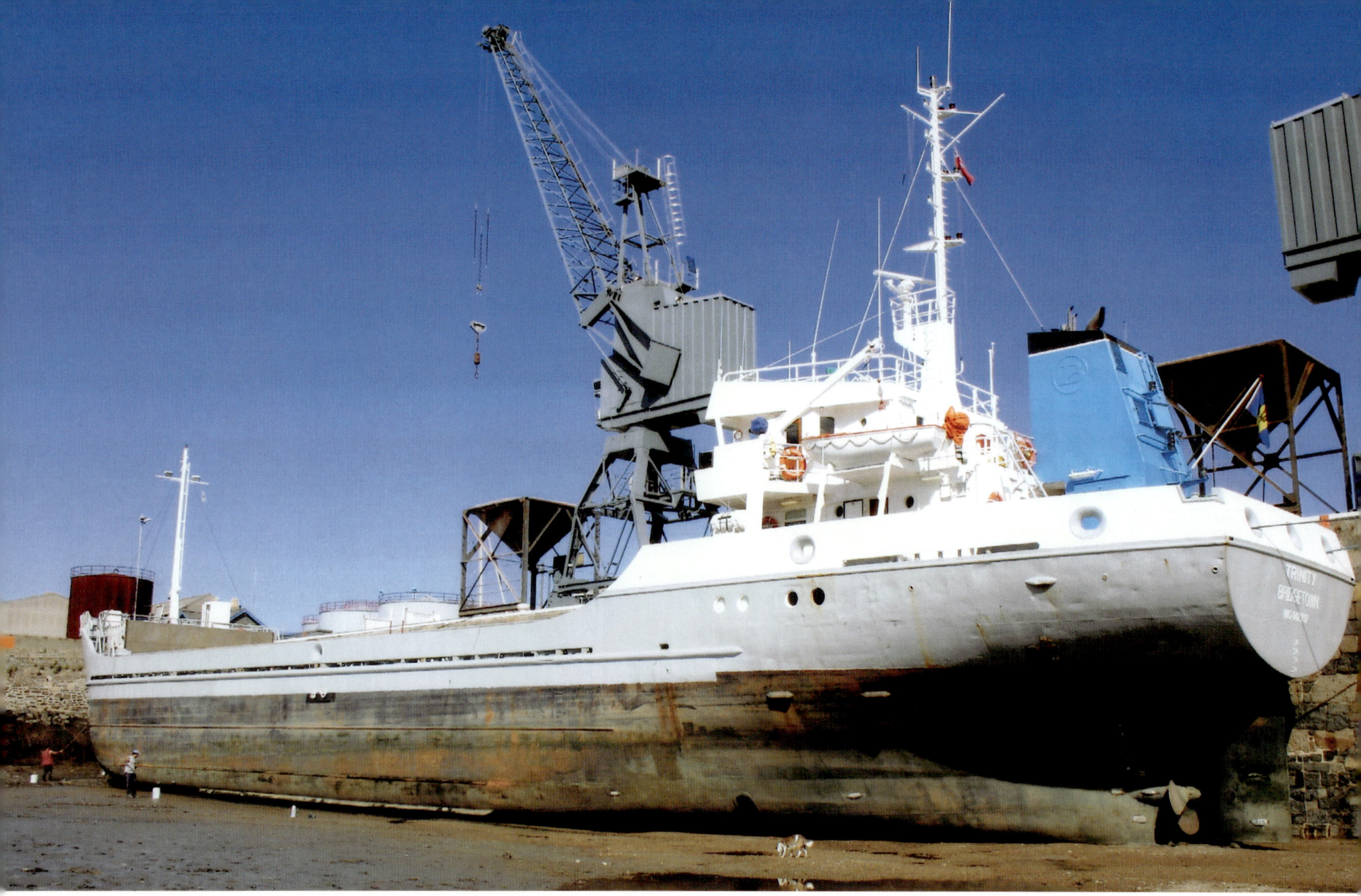

Dried out at St Sampson's and under a clear blue sky, it was a good time for the crew to clean and paint the underwater hull of the ***Trinity*** (BRB, 997gt/86) owned by Faversham Ships Ltd. She had arrived on 17 September 2005 from Llanddulas with a cargo of limestone dust and sailed in ballast next day for Le Légué on the Brittany coast. Formerly owned by the Dutch company Beck's as ***Triton***, she is one of a group of fine coasters built for them by Bodewes of Hoogezand in the 1980s.

(Peter Stewart)

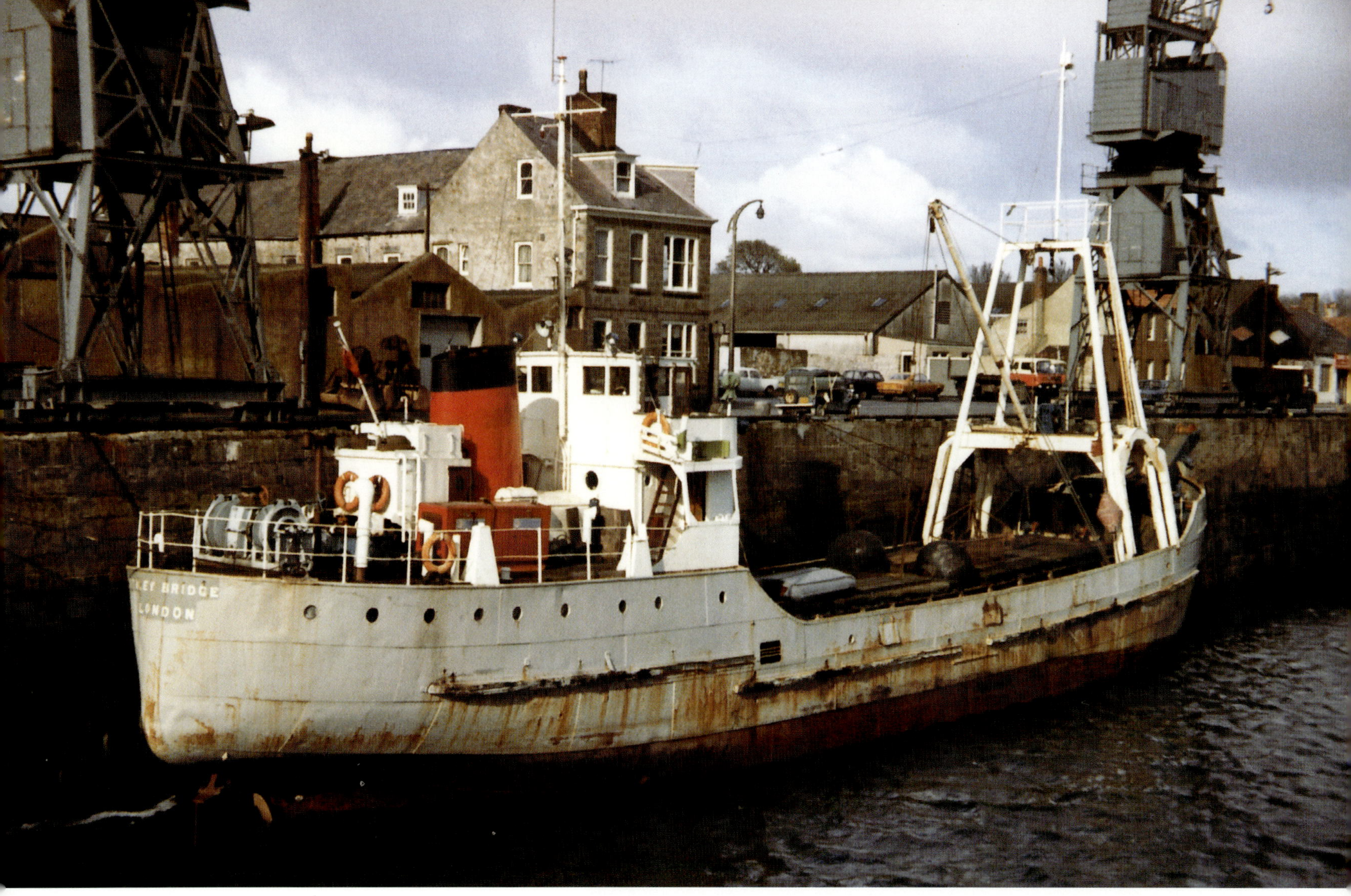

South Side berths at St Sampson's do not lend themselves to good photography except early or late on summer days. This is an early morning view of the ***Staley Bridge*** (GBR, 297grt/40). She was built at Bowling on the River Clyde by Scott & Sons for John Summers, of Shotton in North Wales. After a long career with this owner, she was sold in 1967 to W Wharton, of Liverpool. Two years later, she was acquired by W T Bateman, of Ilford, and a further sale in 1971 saw her bought by Folkestone Salvage Co Ltd and converted for use as a salvage vessel. In 1975, she was bought by J P Rowland, of London, in whose colours she is seen here.

(Derick Goubert)

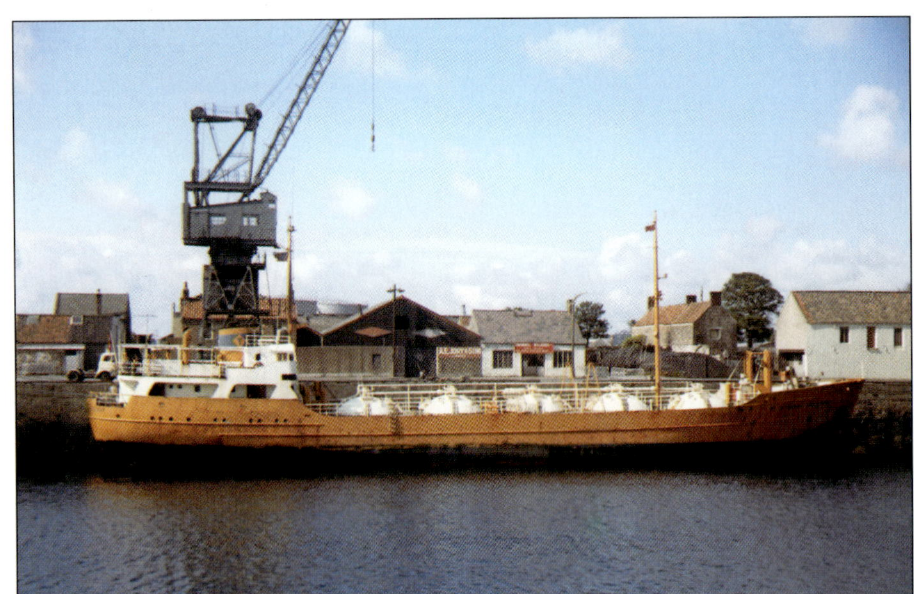

Guernsey's supply of lpg is delivered to St Sampson's. Laid over at an inner berth on the South Side at St Sampson's during the 1970s is the ***Susanne Tholstrup*** (DNK, 394grt/59). She was built by Svendborg Skibsværft and in 1982 was sold to other Danish owners by whom she was renamed ***Karin Grenius***. She was broken up at Naantali in Finland two years later.

(Derick Goubert)

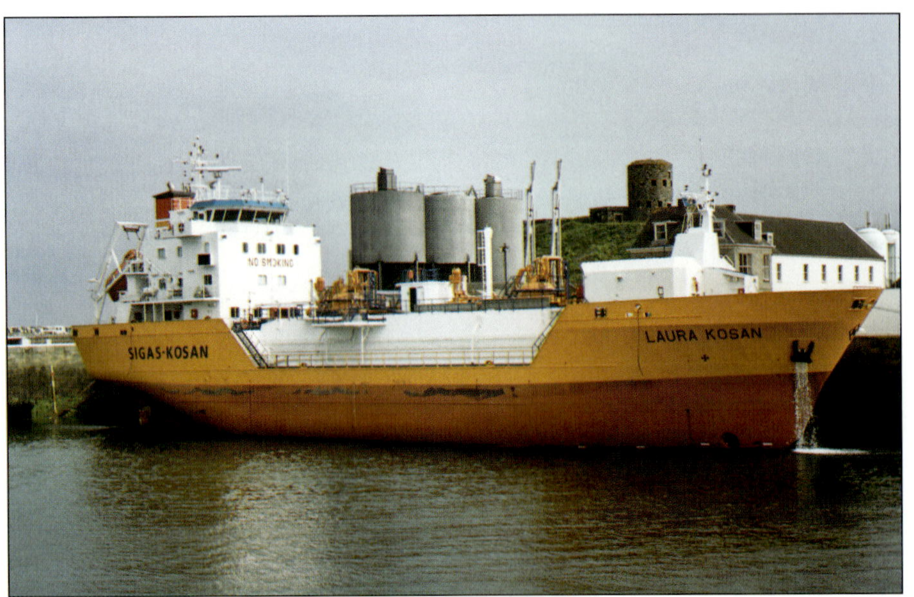

The number of tanker berths which dry out at low water has been steadily reduced over the years. However, the South Side berth at St Sampson's is still very much in use. On 12 July 2002, the ***Laura Kosan*** (IOM, 2223gt/92) is pumping lpg into the white tanks on the right of the photograph. The three grey tanks are bulk cement silos. The stone tower on top of Mont Crevelt is the local version of a Martello tower. The tanker was built at the Hermann Sürken shipyard in Papenburg for Lauritzen Kosan A/S, of Copenhagen.

(Peter Stewart)

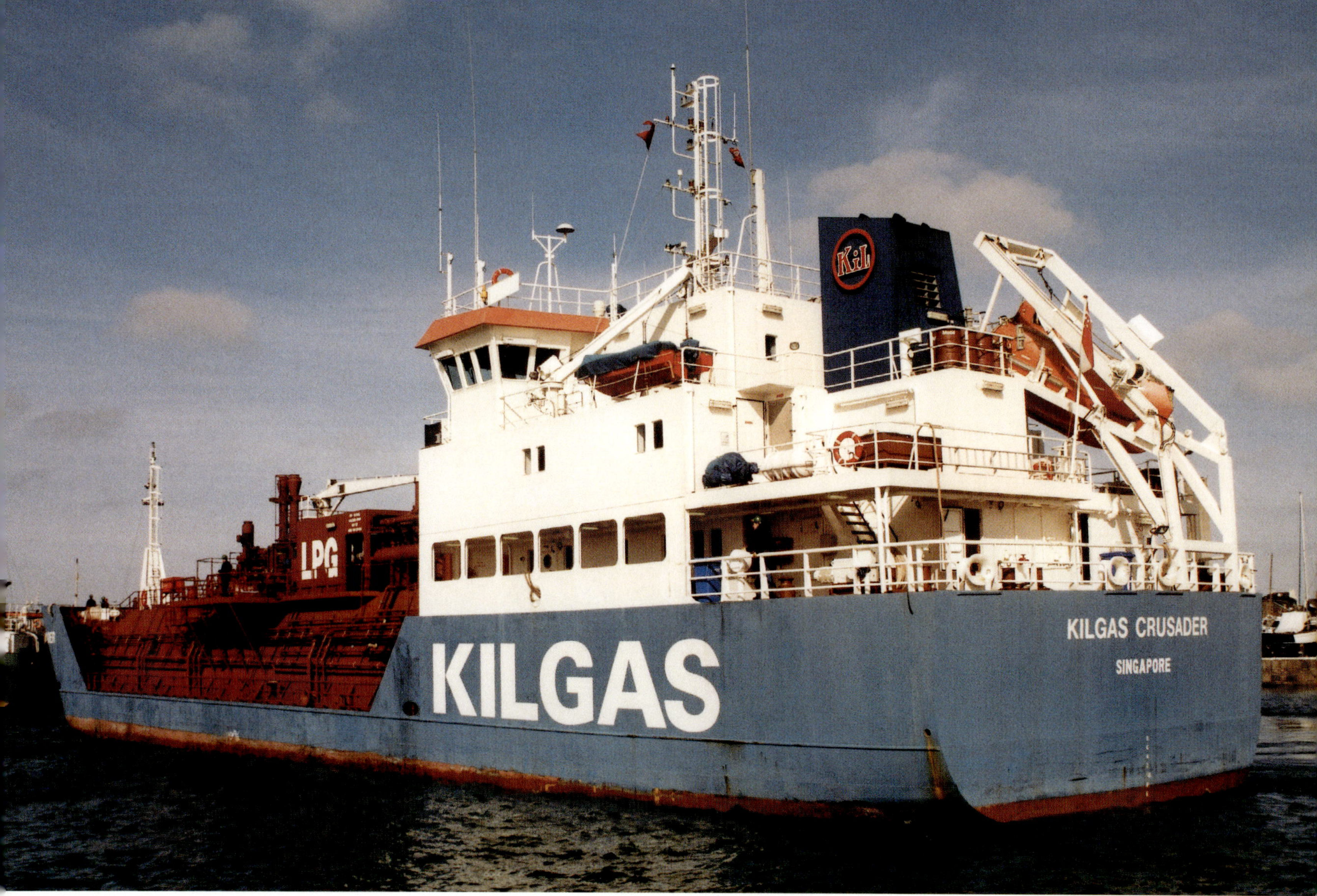

The contract to transport lpg, usually from the Esso refinery at Fawley, has changed hands several times in recent years. In 1999, it was tankers from the Knud I Larsen fleet which were seen and on 22 March that year, the ***Kilgas Crusader*** (SGP, 2458gt/96) is seen arriving at the South Side fuel berth. We have already seen this tanker on page 21 under her later name of ***Sigas Crusader***, acquired in 2001 after the Kilgas fleet had been taken over by Tschudi & Eitzen.

(Peter Stewart)

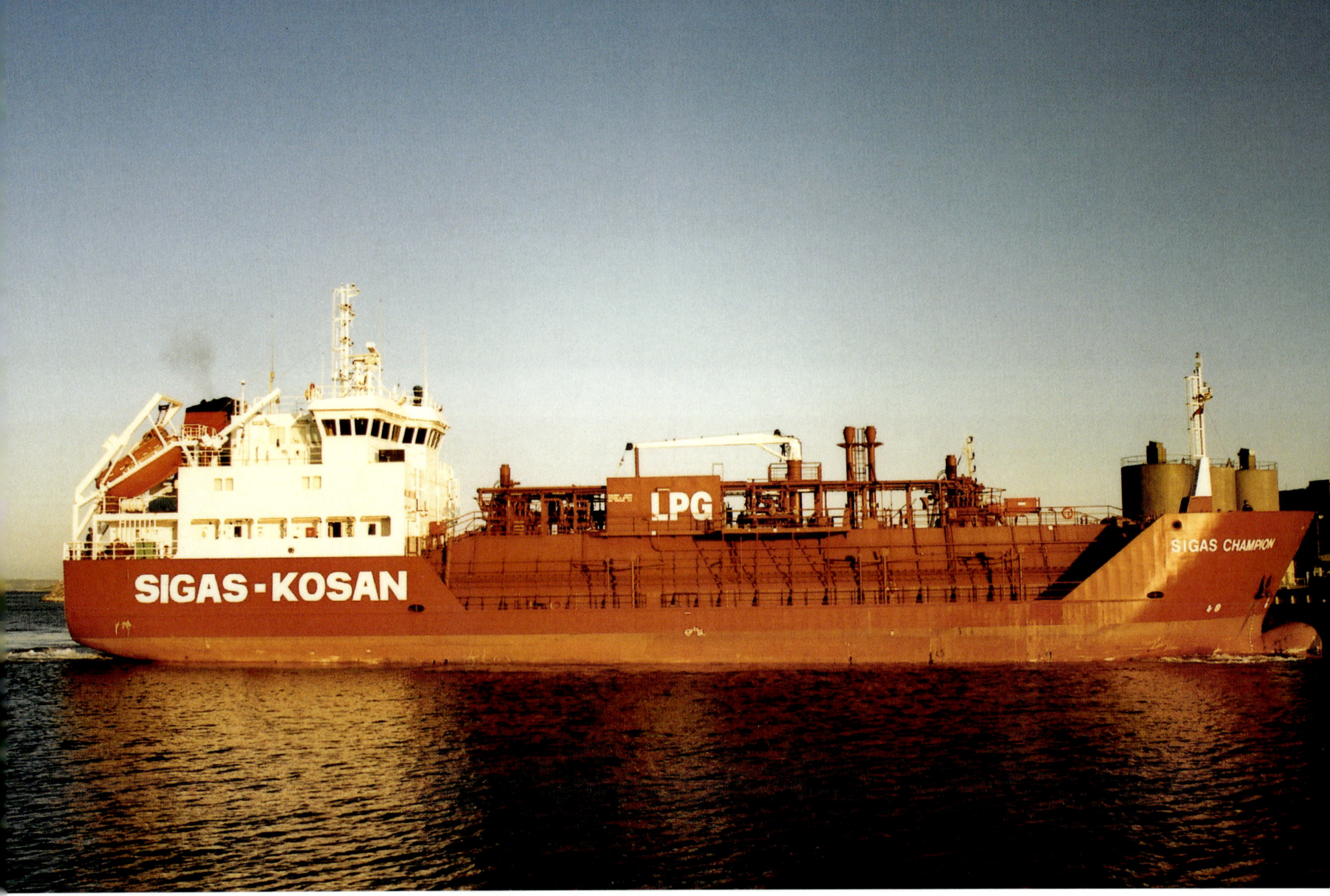

As noted on the previous page, the Kilgas tankers were taken over by Norwegian operator Tschudi & Eitzen in 2001 and some of the tankers joined a pool with Kosan tankers, hence the Sigas - Kosan legend. The ***Sigas Champion*** (SGP, 2458gt/95) is a sistership of the ***Kilgas Crusader*** from the same builder and indeed was called ***Kilgas Champion*** until 2001. She is seen turning off the South Side berth prior to leaving St Sampson's on 25 June 2002.

(Peter Stewart)

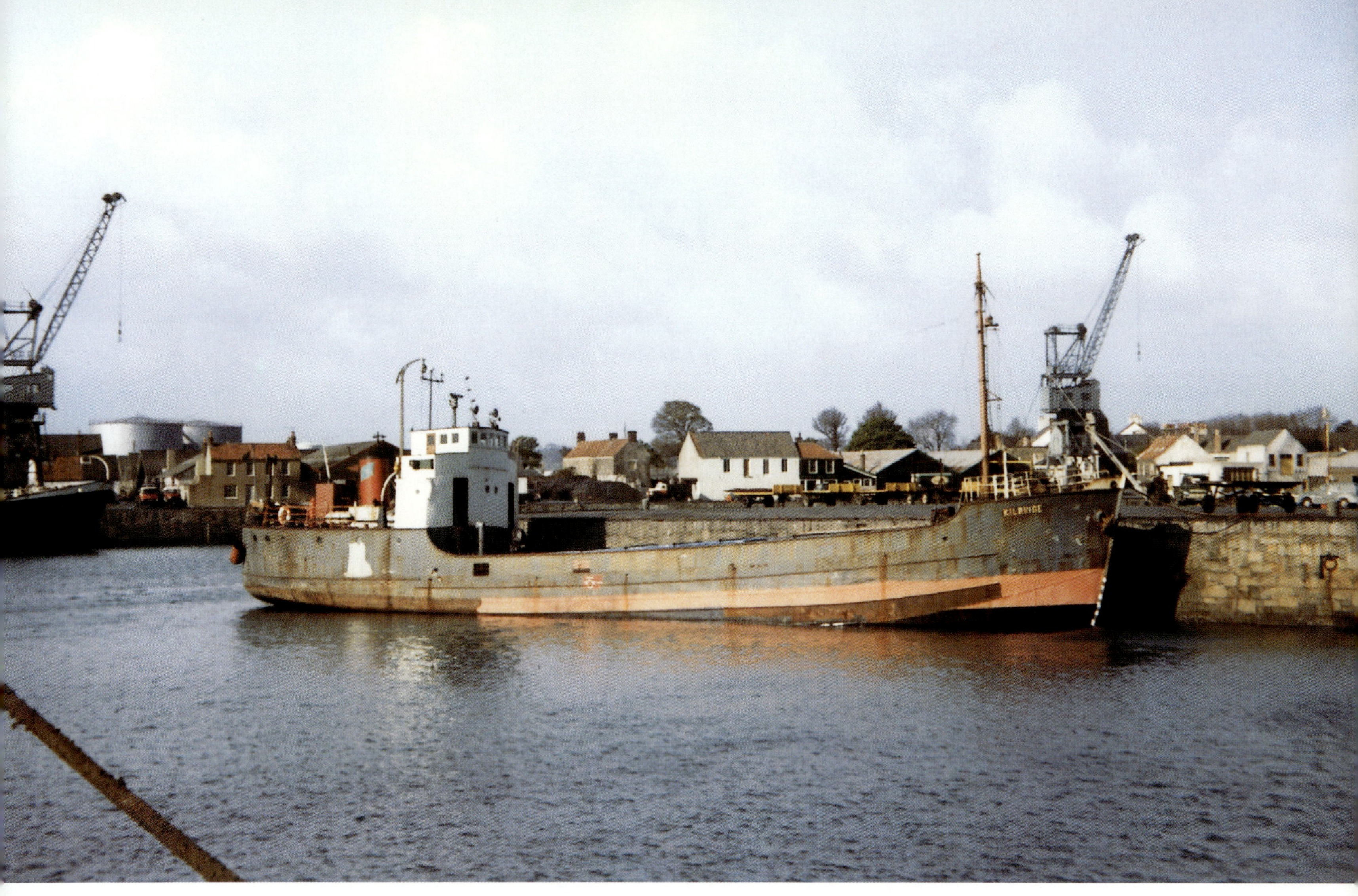

One of the last war-built standard Empire vessels to see service around our coasts was the ***Kilbride*** (IRL, 325grt/42) seen here laid up on the eastern side of the strangely-named Abraham's Bosom in St Sampson's harbour in 1973 when owned in Guernsey by a Mr T Rive. Built at Great Yarmouth as ***Empire Reynard***, the vessel passed to the Dutch Government in 1943 then to French owners in 1946. In 1951 she was sold to R T V Hall, of Dublin, who renamed her ***Kilbride***. By the time she came down to the Channel Islands she was well past her sell-by date and was broken up at Hull during 1974.

(Derick Goubert)

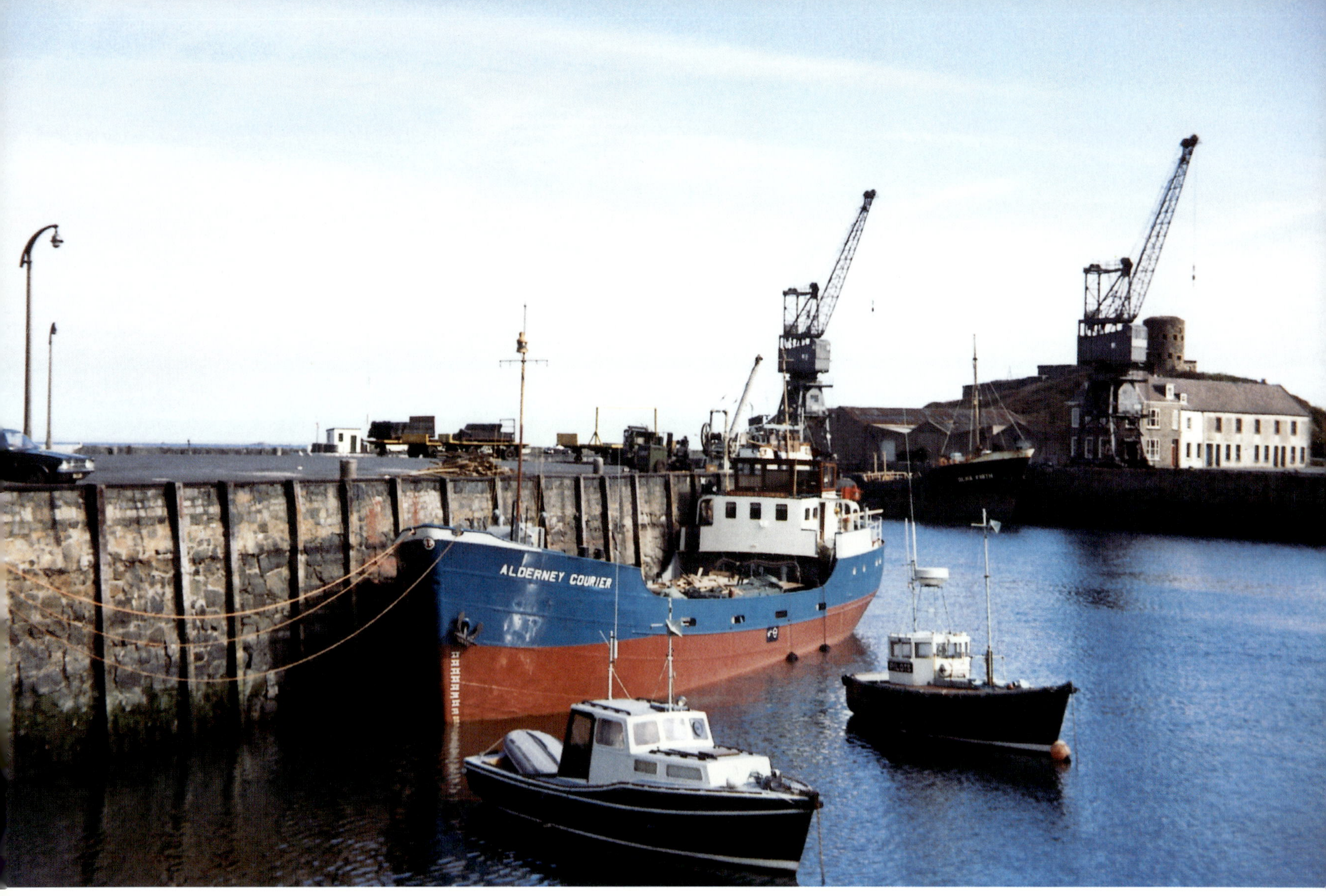

Berthed on the inside of Abraham's Bosom in St Sampson's is the ***Alderney Courier*** (GBR, 203grt/40) of Link Services Ltd. She was built by Scheepswerf Delfzijl v/h Sander as ***Tasman***, becoming ***Wim*** in 1941, ***Capricorn*** in 1954, ***Rejo*** in 1955, ***Wilca*** in 1956, ***Reiger*** in 1965, and ***Alderney Courier*** in 1970. She was wrecked in the West Indies sometime during the 1980s.

(Derick Goubert)

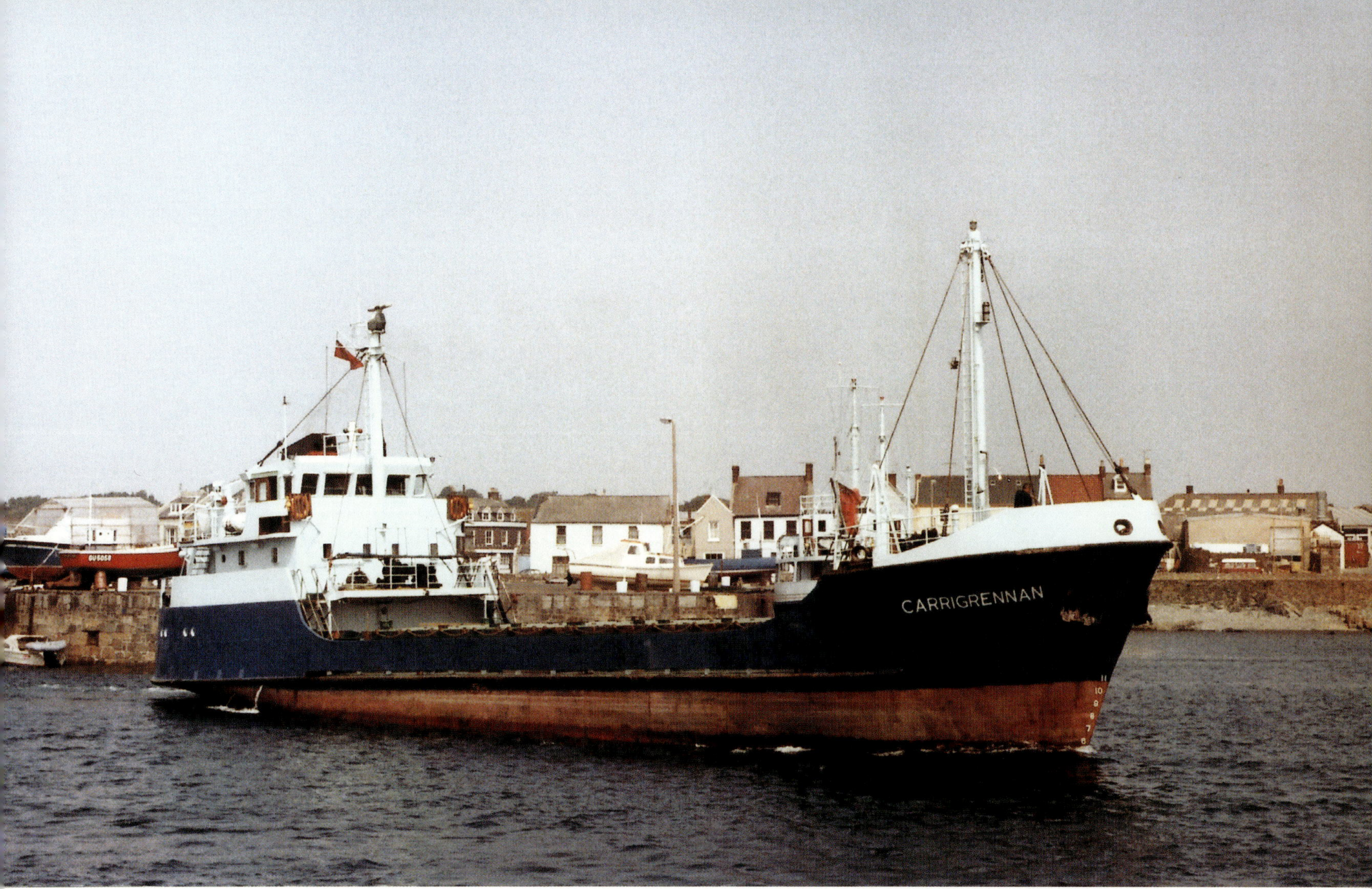

Heading out of St Sampson's in ballast possibly bound for St Peter Port to load supplies for Alderney, the ***Carrigrennan*** (GBR, 387grt/70) was owned at the time by Alderney Shipping Ltd. The quayside is Abraham's Bosom and was used until the early 1970s for discharging and stacking timber. Coasters were unloaded using their own derricks. It served also as lay-up berth or for vessels under repair. Nowadays it is only used for the wintering and refitting of fishing and pleasure boats. Built at Cork by Verolme Cork Dockyard Ltd as ***Darell*** for the Tyrrell family, of Arklow, she was the last coaster specially built to fit the lock into Ringsend Dock in Dublin. In 1989, she was sold to a Canadian owner and renamed ***Free Trade***. In 1994, her name became ***Mother Wood***. She is believed to be still in service though now flying the flag of Panama and owned in Haiti.

(Derick Goubert)

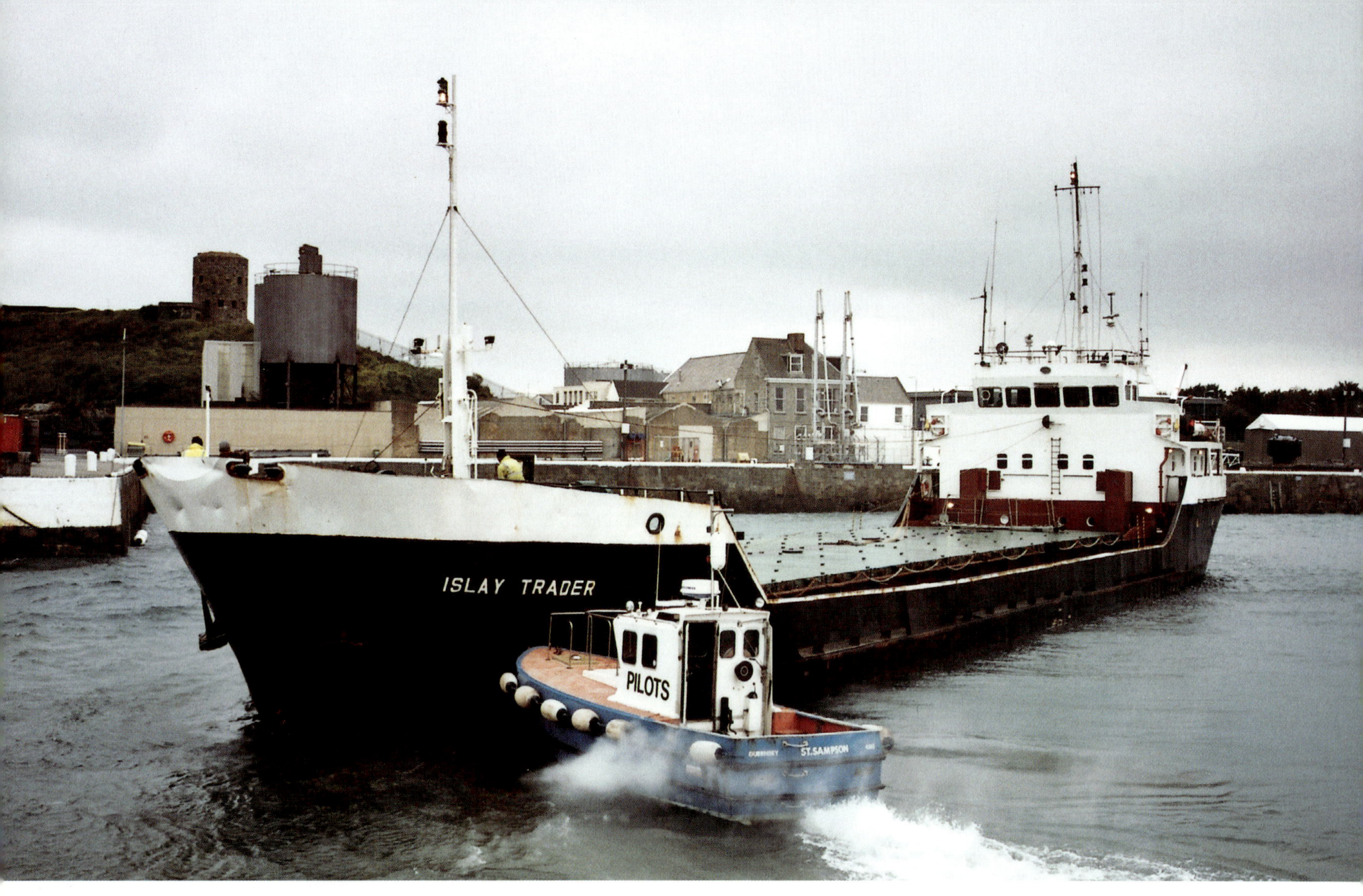

Here we see the ***Islay Trader*** (BRB, 909gt/80), ex ***Sea Kestrel***-03, ***Pentland***-00, ***Capacity***-94, ***Lizzonia***-89, backing away from a North Side berth at St Sampson's assisted by the local pilot cutter ***St Sampson*** on a very dull 10 October 2004. She was bound for Dunkerque with scrap metal. Owned by Faversham Ships Ltd, she was built by Cochrane Shipbuilders Ltd at Selby. Shortly after this photograph was taken, she was sold to Italian operators Soc Cooperative de Navegationie G. Guiliette a. r. l. who renamed her ***Sea Star*** still under the Barbados flag.

(Peter Stewart)

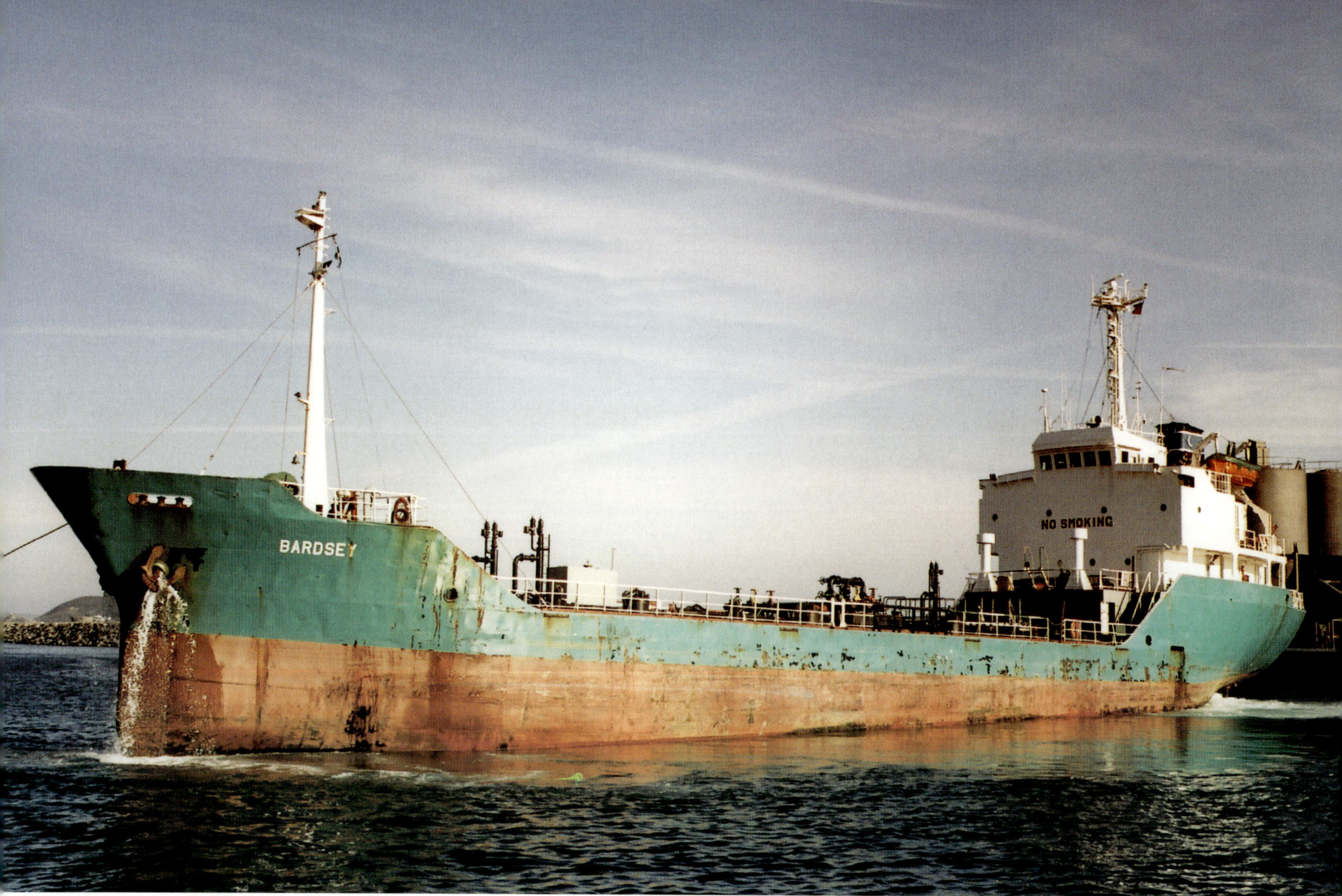

Highlighted in the evening sunshine of 25 April 2002, the hull of Crescent Marine Services' tanker ***Bardsey*** (GBR, 1144gt/81), ex ***Sten***-86, is painted in the (thankfully) short-lived green. She is turning in St Sampson's harbour having discharged fuel oils on the South Side for Esso from Fawley refinery on Southampton Water. The ***Bardsey*** was one of four Japanese tankers sent to European waters in the early 1980s on charter and later sold, two each to Crescent and Everards. All have now been sold on to other foreign owners. The ***Bardsey*** was renamed ***Magadir*** after being bought by Mediterranean owners in autumn 2005. Her builder was Kitanihou Zosen KK, of Hachinote.

(Peter Stewart)

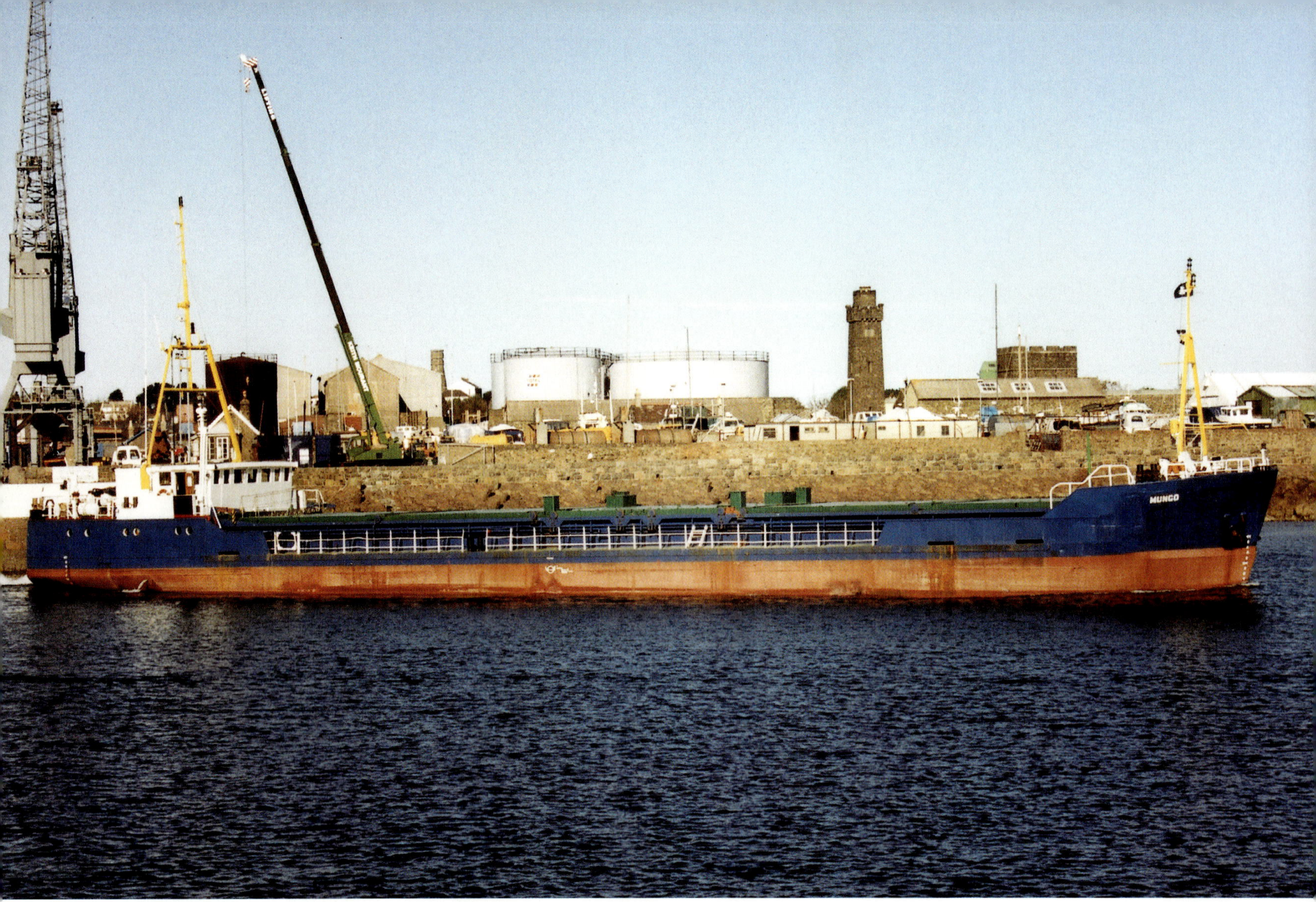

Sailing from St Sampson's on a beautiful sunny 5 November 2001, the ***Mungo*** (BHS, 664gt/80) has unloaded a cargo of building sand from Shoreham and she is now bound for Poole where she will load a further sand cargo for Guernsey. Along with the ***Pongo***, her registered owners are Ortac Ltd. Although a sister ship to ***Pongo***, she was built in Denmark by A/S Nordsøværftet at Ringkøbing. Her regular Master has been Derick Goubert since he sold his ***Candourity***.

(Peter Stewart)

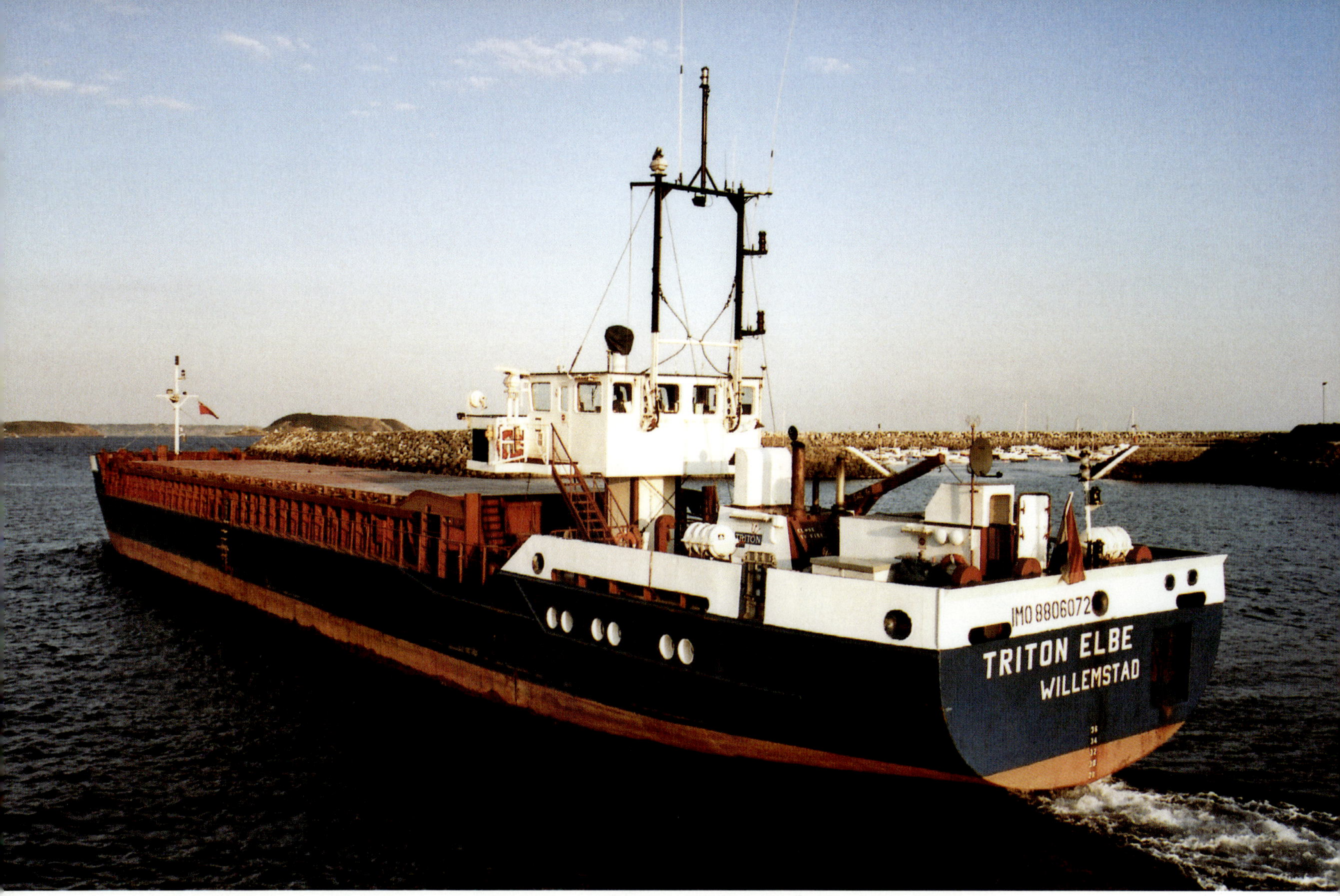

Outward bound from St Sampson's on the beautifully clear evening of 6 July 2004, the ***Triton Elbe*** (ANT, 910gt/88) had brought a cargo of limestone aggregate from Llanddulas and is sailing to Plymouth for a further cargo of limestone for Guernsey, returning three days later. Behind is the reclaimed area to the south of the harbour mouth, and to the left the smaller islands of Jethou, Sark, and Herm. She is a product of Cassens yard in Emden and was named ***Sea Danube*** until 1995 and then ***Howden*** until 1999.

(Peter Stewart)

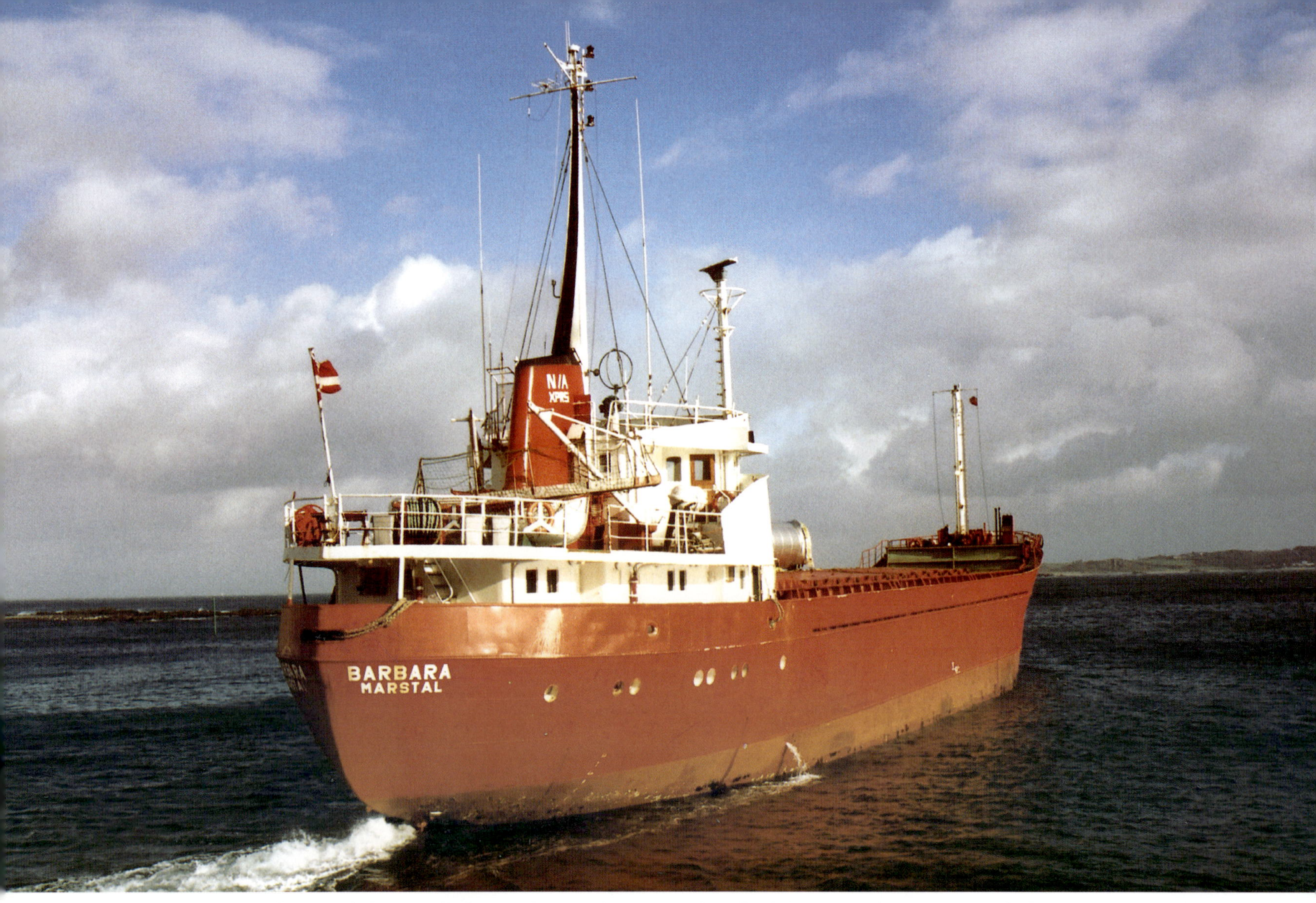

Here we see the ***Barbara*** (DIS, 1068gt/66) leaving St Sampson's on 28 January 2003 having arrived from Esbjerg with an unusual cargo of exhaust flues and fittings for the local power station. However several items proved too heavy for the dockside cranes so she then made the half hour sailing to St Peter Port for them to be unloaded and taken by road back to St Sampson's. Built as ***Regine*** by the J J Sietas shipyard on the outskirts of Hamburg, she is a variant of its Type 33 semi-container vessel with a capacity of 52 TEU.

(Peter Stewart)

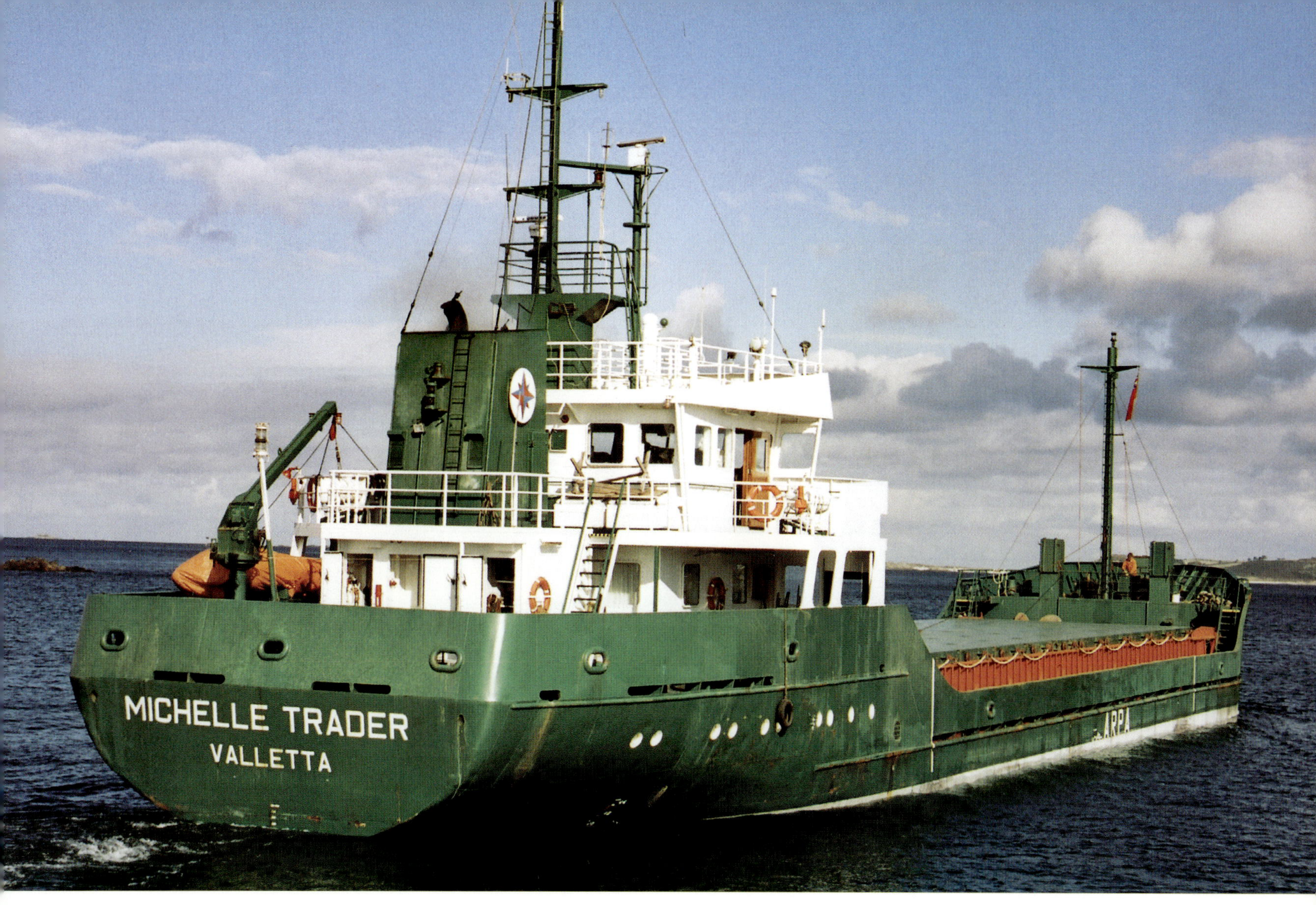

One of the many coasters operated under the ARPA banner, the ***Michelle Trader*** (MLT, 994gt/83) owned by M T Shipping Ltd, of Valletta, leaves St Sampson's for the north Spanish port of El Ferrol with scrap metal on 30 August 2001. She was built as ***Paul Brinkman*** by E J Smit & Zoon's yard at Westerbroek for Brinkman Beheer B.V., of Groningen. In 1988 she was renamed ***Paola***, her owners being Frigga Shipping Co Ltd, of Limassol, but still retained her Dutch connections with Brinkman.

(Peter Stewart)

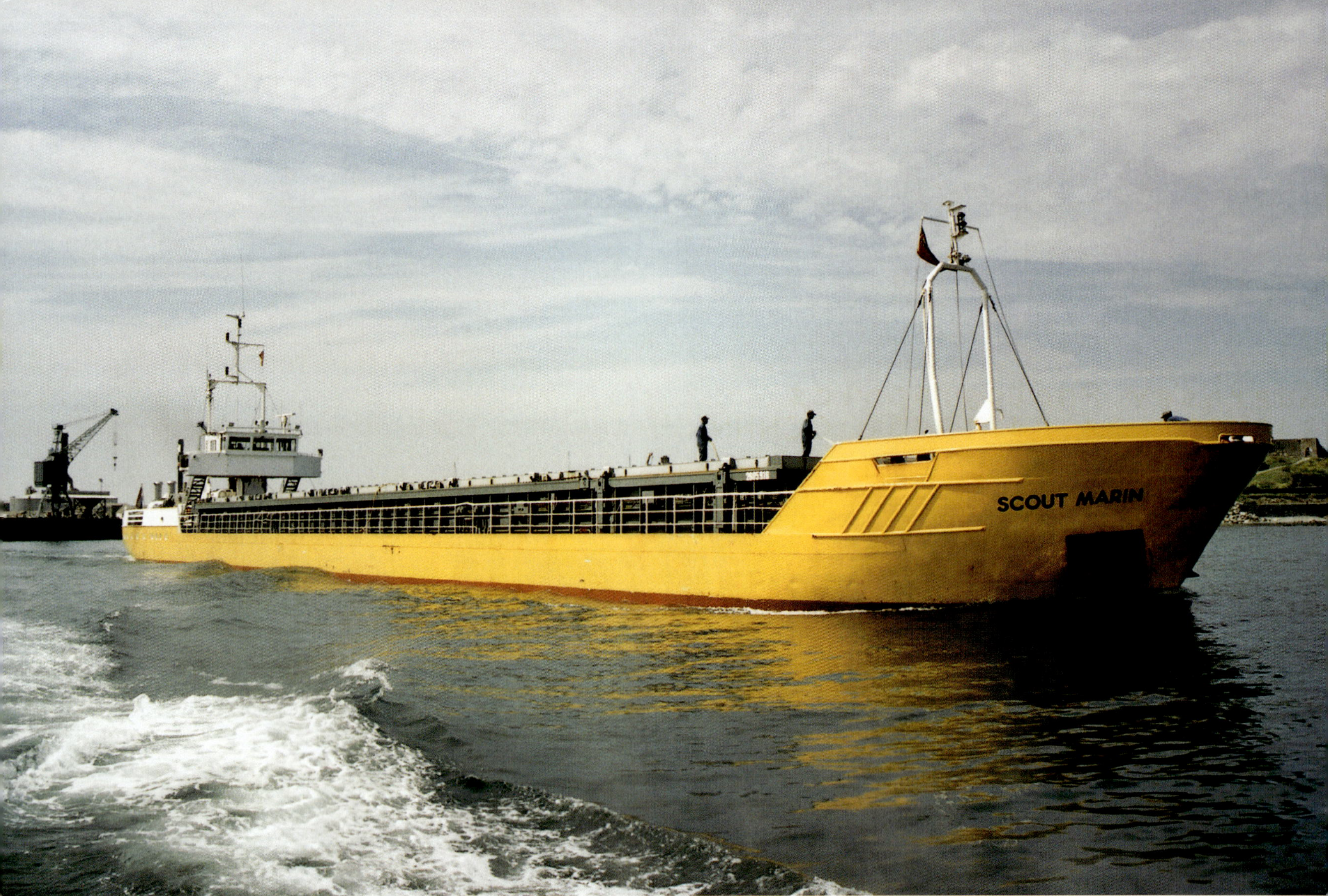

Taken from the St Sampson's pilot cutter, this is a fine view of the strikingly coloured ***Scout Marin*** (NLD, 1035gt/83) when outward bound for El Ferrol with a full cargo of scrap metal on 19 July 2002. The ***Scout Marin*** was built at Oldersum by Julius Diedrich Schiffswerft as ***Wilke*** for Briese Schiffahrts KG, of Emden. Between 1988 and 1989 she was named ***Sea Dart*** while on charter to Seacon Ltd, of London, and she was sold in 1993 to Capt Jan de Jonge, of Meppel, and hoisted the Dutch flag.

(Peter Stewart)

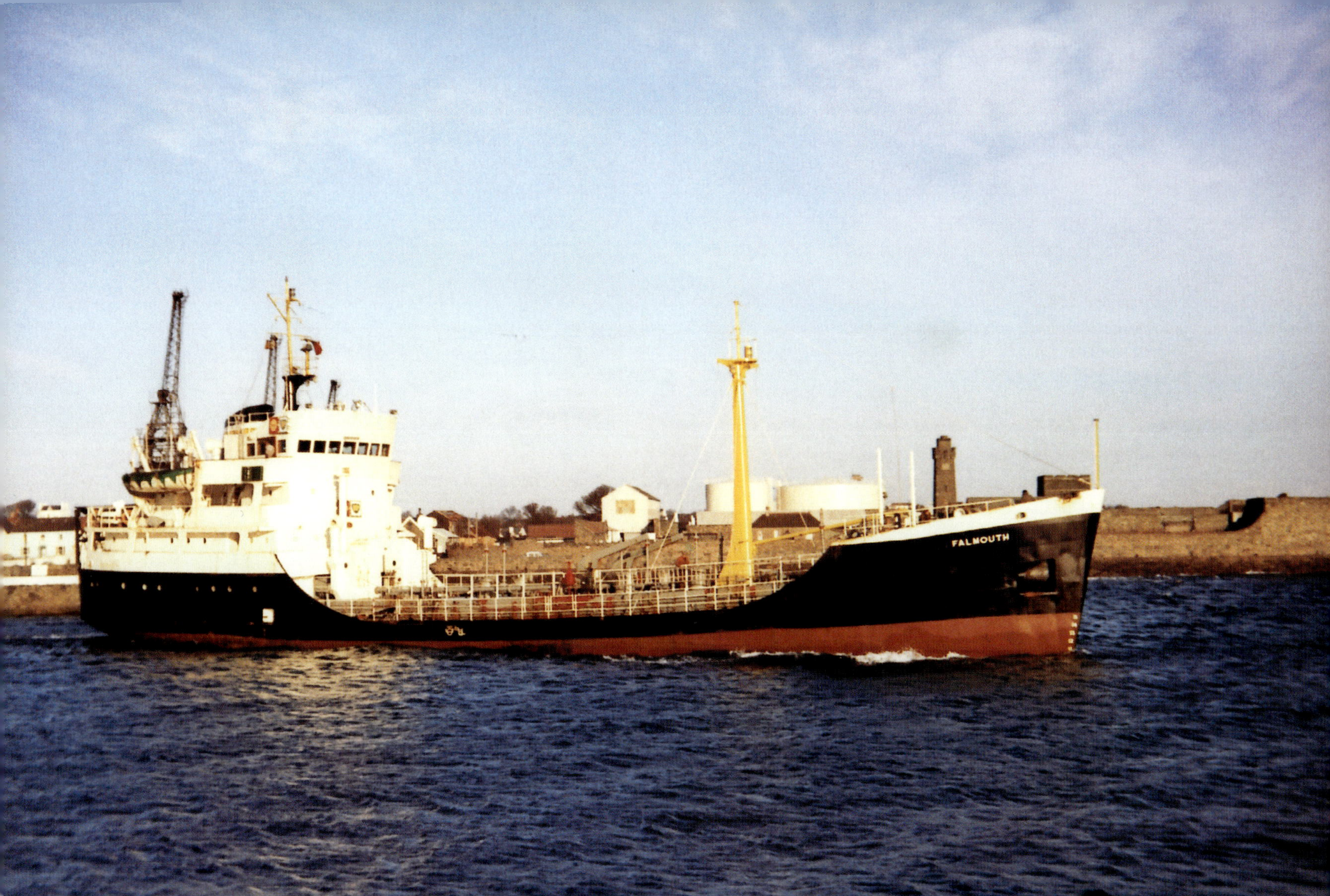

A smart looking ***Falmouth*** (GBR, 982grt/65) leaves St Sampson's on a sunny morning in the 1970s. She was one of a pair built by Grangemouth Dockyard in 1965 for Shell Mex & BP Ltd. She became ***Shell Mariner*** in 1980 before being sold to Canadian owners Coastal Shipping Ltd in 1982 but still registered in London and renamed ***Jennie W***. She passed to Panamanian flag owners as ***Orfeo*** in 1994.

(Derick Goubert)

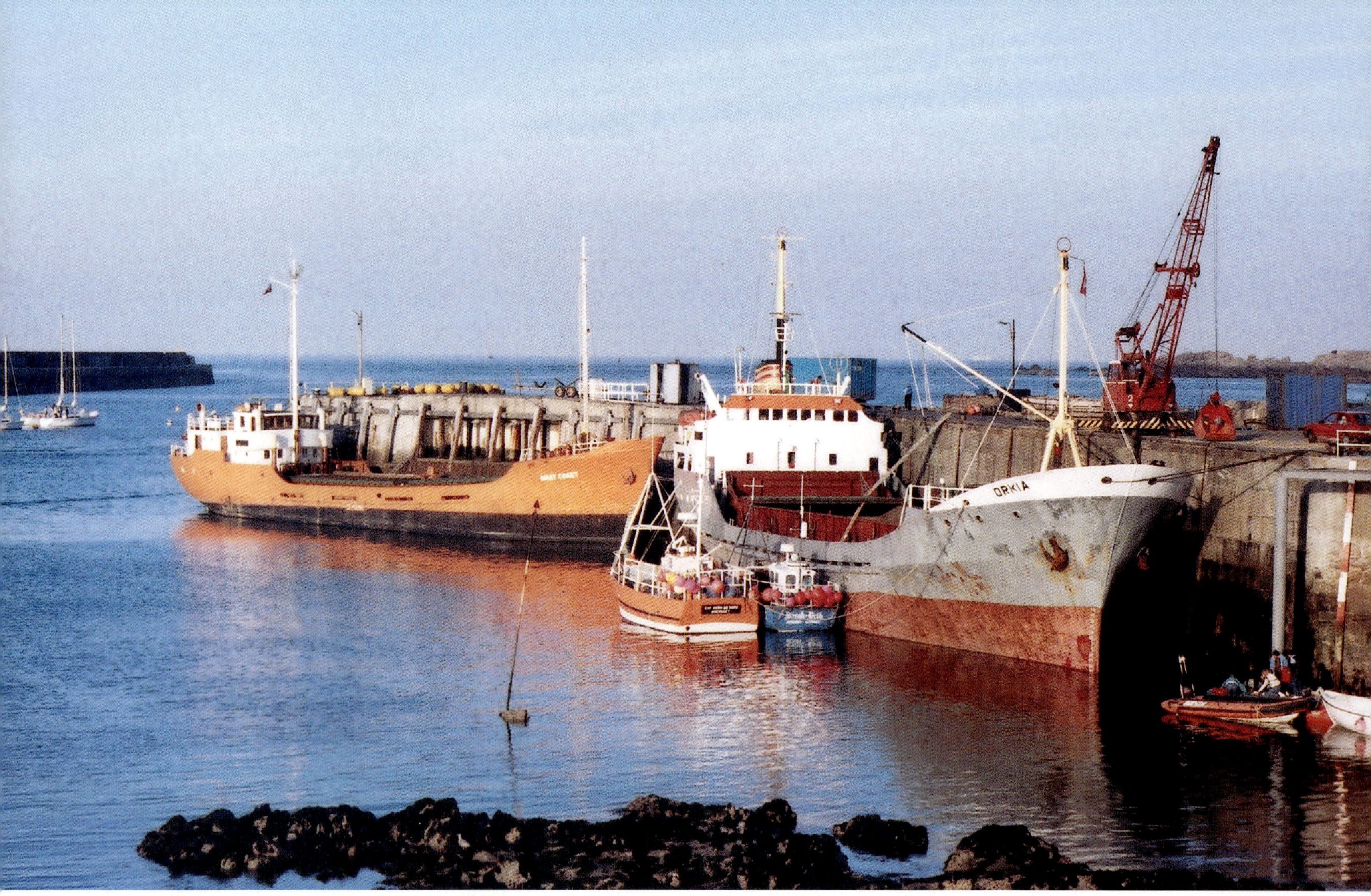

We now look briefly at the only other two Channel Islands to be visited by coasters. Alderney's Braye Harbour is seen on a fine summer evening with two vessels alongside. Harris & Dixon's Spanish-built ***Orkia*** (GBR, 750grt/76) was loading gravel and Derick Goubert's ***Mary Coast*** (GBR, 386grt/61) was on the general cargo run from Guernsey in the late 1980s. This jetty is soon to be rebuilt and extended to accommodate larger coasters. The largest ships able to berth here are Everard's tankers of the ***Activity*** type at 79,3 m long which bring fuel oil for Alderney's power station. The ***Orkia***, ex ***Urkia***-86, ***Danis***-87, was built by S.A. Balenciaga at Zumaya in Spain. She was renamed ***Orkia II*** in 1991.

(Derick Goubert)

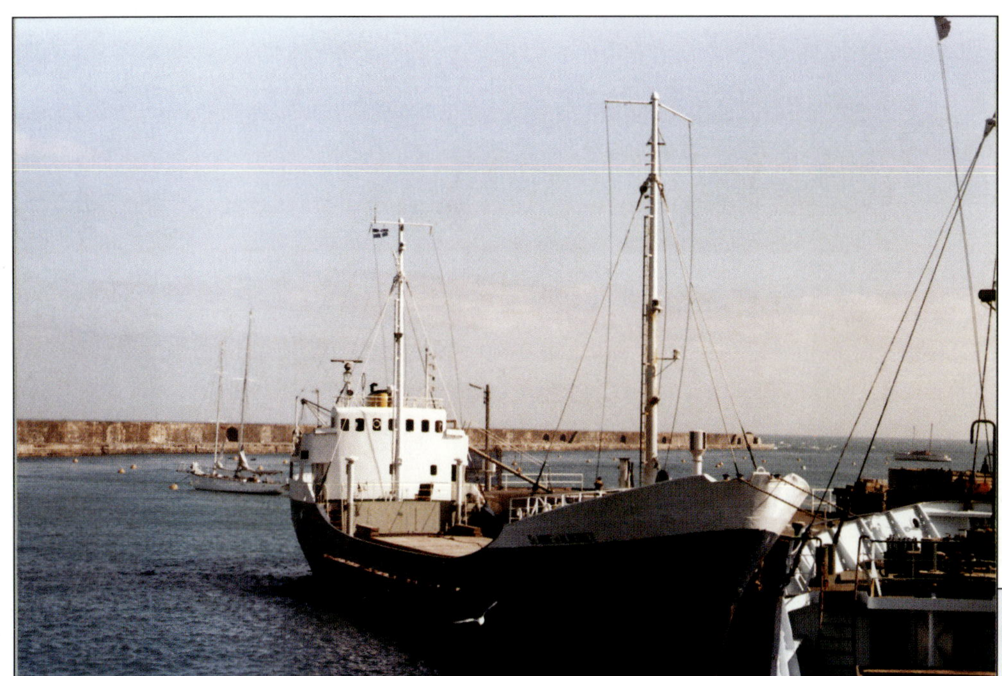

The appropriately-named ***St Anne of Alderney*** (GBR, 300grt/63), owned locally at the time by Hurd Deep Shipping Ltd, is seen in Braye harbour with the port's huge breakwater in the background. Built at Ørskovs Staalskibsværft in Frederikshavn as ***Jens Rand***, this coaster later became ***Juto*** and ***Baltzborg*** before being sold to her Channel Islands owner in late 1979. The intention was to operate a cargo service from Plymouth to the island along with general tramping. This was not successful and she was sold to Caribbean owners, becoming simply ***St Anne*** in 1986. She is still listed in the current *Lloyd's Register*.

(Derick Goubert)

Much of Alderney's cargo is now carried in containers and the two small container carriers of Alderney Shipping Ltd, the ***Isis*** and ***Burhou I***, are now the most frequent callers usually on a weekly basis. On the right we have a stern view of the ***Isis*** discharging on 23 August 2000.

(Dave Hocquard)

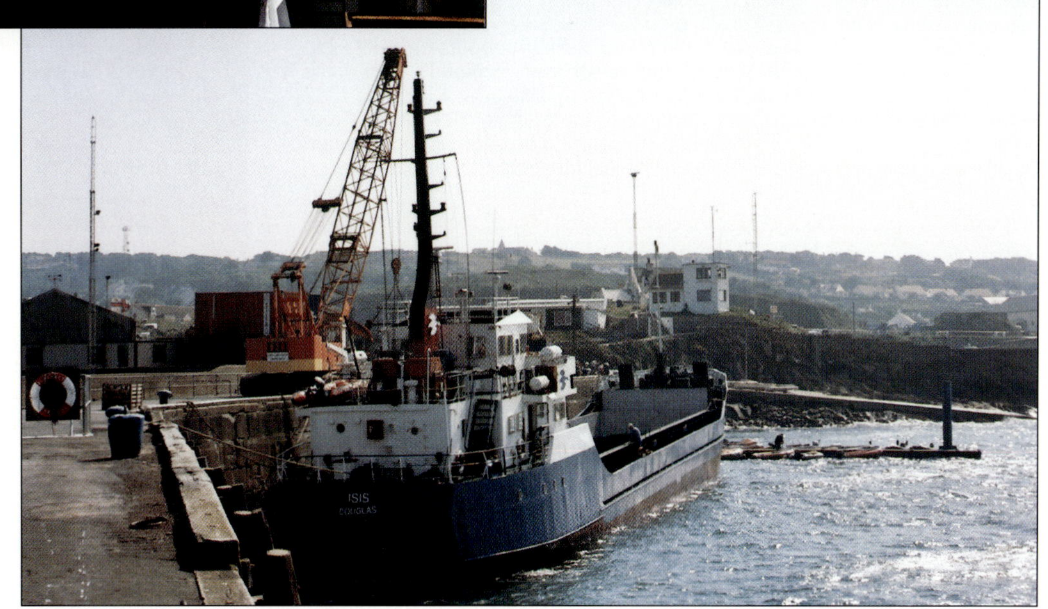

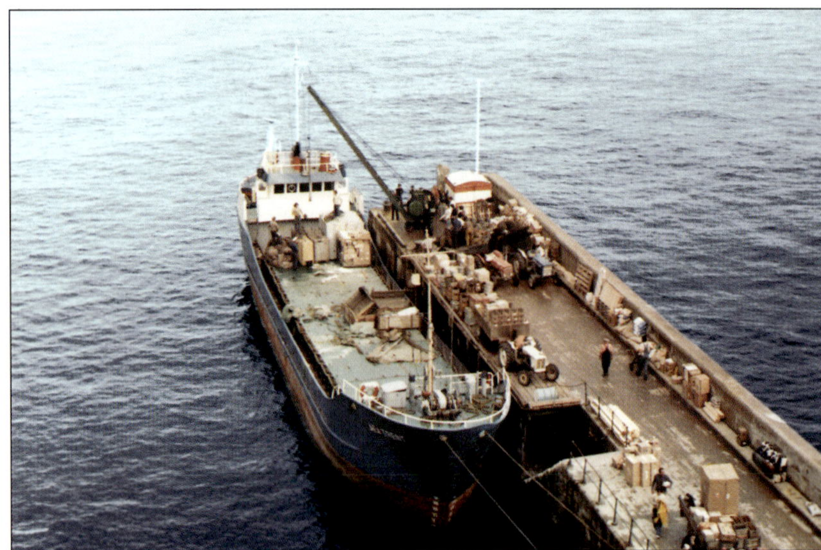

Above : Taken from the cliff top between Creux and La Maseline harbours in Sark, this fine view shows Alderney Shipping Co's ***Sea Trent*** (GBR, 200grt/68) discharging cargo using the harbour's small hand crane probably in 1973 or 1974; this was hard and slow work. It is very rare to see a coaster in one of Sark's harbours but until 1939 very small coasters would bring cargoes of coal direct from England's east coast ports each winter. The ***Sea Trent*** was the Alderney supply ship from 1973 until 1982 when she was sold to German owners for a service to the island of Heligoland. From 1986 to date and now named ***Silver River***, she is usually to be seen sailing between Glasson Dock, near Lancaster, and the Isle of Man for Mezeron Ltd, of Ramsey.

(Derick Goubert)

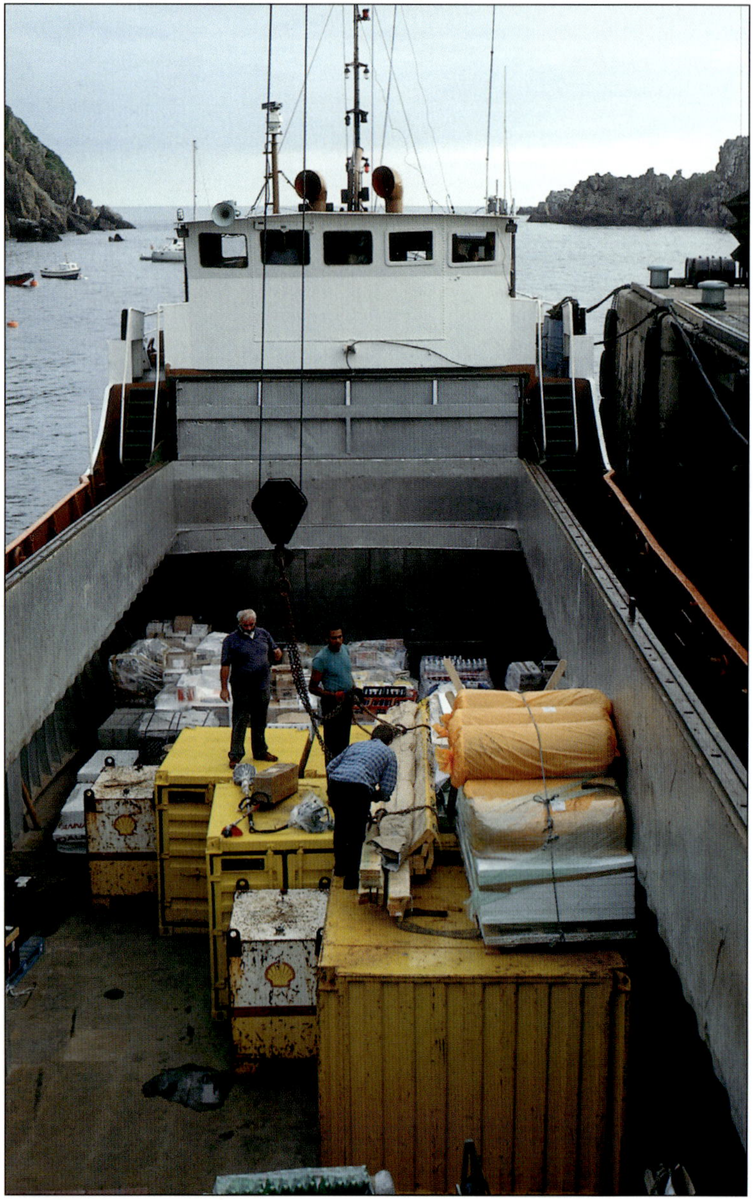

Right : Derick Goubert's ***Port Soif*** (GBR, 429grt/71) is thought to have been the largest vessel to have delivered cargo to Sark.Taken during a call at the island in July 1993, this photograph illustrates the varied general cargo required to maintain the island. Building materials, household goods and various liquid refreshments can be clearly seen. This attractive coaster was built at the Gebr. Coops shipyard in Hoogezand as ***Camilla Weston***. In 1984, she was sold and renamed ***Delce*** and took the name ***Port Soif*** following purchase by Captain Goubert in 1990. On 22 December 1993, she grounded near the island of Herm. After a period laid up at Oreston Quay, Plymouth, and on the slipway at Ramsgate in 1994, she was sold for service in the West Indies as ***Bahamas Provider***.

(Bernard McCall)